# Jane Austen
# and her World
# Josephine Ross

Published in Great Britain by National Portrait Gallery Publications,
National Portrait Gallery, St Martin's Place, London WC2H 0HE

For a complete catalogue of current publications please write to the
address above, or visit our website at www.npg.org.uk/publications

First published 2017

ISBN 978 1 85514 701 0

A catalogue record for this book is available from the British Library.

10 9 8 7 6 5 4 3 2 1

Managing Editor: Christopher Tinker
Copy-editor: Helen Armitage
Design: Smith & Gilmour
Picture research: Mark Lynch
Production: Ruth Müller-Wirth
Printed and bound in Hong Kong

The publisher would like to thank the copyright holders for granting
permission to reproduce works illustrated in this book. Every effort
has been made to contact the holders of copyright material, and
any omissions will be corrected in future editions if the publisher
is notified in writing.

Sold to support the National Portrait Gallery, London

# Contents

# 'THE CRADLE OF HER GENIUS'

'It was at Steventon that the real foundations
of her fame were laid.'
A Memoir of Jane Austen, J.E. Austen-Leigh, 1870

'I dearly love a laugh.'
Elizabeth Bennet, in Pride and Prejudice, 1813

Towards the end of 1813, writing to her sister Cassandra,
Jane Austen indulged in some playful speculation about the
effects the modest success of her latest novel, Pride and Prejudice,
might have upon her life and prospects. Published in January of
that year, in a small edition of some 1,500 copies, 'P.&P.' (as she
called it) had already been reprinted, having earned several
favourable reviews and been well received by the public. 'I do not
despair of having my picture in the Exhibition at last,' she wrote
with mock self-importance, 'all white & red, with my Head on
one Side.' It was a characteristic Jane Austen joke.

There was, indeed, a little watercolour sketch of her fitting
that description, which Cassandra had done some years earlier,
and the family had kept, although it was considered a poor
likeness. But such an amateur image of an obscure country
'authoress' could, of course, have no place on display among

...........
OPPOSITE
**Jane Austen**
Cassandra Austen, c.1810

# PRIDE

### AND

# PREJUDICE:

## A NOVEL.

*IN THREE VOLUMES.*

———————

BY THE

AUTHOR OF " SENSE AND SENSIBILITY."

———————

VOL. I.

━━━━━━━

London:

PRINTED FOR T. EGERTON,
MILITARY LIBRARY, WHITEHALL.

1813.

portraits of the famous and fashionable by leading artists such as Sir Joshua Reynolds – whose recent retrospective in Pall Mall Jane had seen during a trip to London. 'I had great amusement among the Pictures,' she had told Cassandra after visiting that exhibition, and another of watercolours. However, there was one disappointment: 'There was nothing like Mrs. D.,' she wrote, 'at either.' Playfully, she had expressed high hopes of seeing a portrait of Elizabeth Bennet, heroine of *Pride and Prejudice*, who had married the novel's hero, Mr Darcy – but with no success. 'I can only imagine that Mr. D. prizes any Picture of her too much to like it should be exposed to the public eye,' she concluded.

In that 'feeling', which she attributed to a 'mixture of Love, Pride & Delicacy' on Mr Darcy's part, Jane Austen was entirely in sympathy with her fictional character. To be 'exposed to the public eye', like an exotic animal in the famous Exeter Exchange menagerie, was a situation she herself was determined to avoid at all costs. Like its predecessor, *Sense and Sensibility* (1811), 'P.&P.' had been published anonymously, and when, some months after its appearance, her brother Henry disclosed what she called 'the Secret' of her authorship to some aristocratic friends, she was deeply distressed. 'A Thing once set going in that way, one knows how it spreads!' she complained. Nevertheless she tried to resign herself to the situation, remarking philosophically, 'If I am a wild Beast, I cannot help it.'

By the time *Mansfield Park* came out, in the following year, she was almost ready to abandon her principles and 'rather try to make', she wrote wryly, 'all the Money, than all the Mystery I can of it'. But discretion, and 'Delicacy', prevailed, and it was not until December 1817, five months after her death, when *Northanger Abbey* and *Persuasion* were published together in a four-volume set, that her name appeared for the first time on any of her novels. The addition of a preface by Henry (a 'Biographical Notice of the Author') revealed not only her identity but also personal details of her life and career, from her looks and literary tastes, love of dancing and dread of 'notoriety' to her last, moving, deathbed words. The 'Thing' Jane Austen so feared, and resisted, had been set going. But just how far it would spread, not even she, in her wildest and wittiest imaginings, could ever have envisaged.

Today, the Hampshire vicar's daughter who died unmarried 200 years ago, aged forty-one, unknown to the public and having made barely £650 from her writing, is famous throughout the world. Her six great novels – and even juvenile works – are constantly filmed, televised, translated and reprinted; studied as classic texts, and re-created in new genres; her total earnings are incalculable. Her opening line from *Pride and Prejudice*, 'It is a truth universally acknowledged', has entered the language; her face is on Britain's coins and banknotes. And her little portrait by Cassandra is now on display at the National Portrait Gallery in London, seen annually by some 2 million visitors.

# Background

Although the name 'Jane Austen' has become synonymous with the world of the Regency – replete, in the popular imagination, with high-waisted dresses and high-sprung phaetons, Napoleonic battlefields and Romantic, Byronic heroes – the life into which she was born, on 16 December 1775, was the more prosaic one of the respectable, rural Georgian gentry: financially secure, socially unpretentious and relatively untroubled by international events. The first battle of the American War of Independence had taken place at Bunker Hill on 17 June 1775, six months before her birth; in France, unrest against the oppressive ruling classes was rising, fuelled by the works of writers and thinkers such as Voltaire and Jean-Jacques Rousseau. But in Britain, King George III still seemed secure on his throne after 15 years. Although constantly lampooned by the cartoonists, and opposed by the Whigs and radicals, he was as yet unaffected by debilitating mental illness, and generally regarded as a stabilising influence, with his love for his plain wife Queen Charlotte and their fifteen children, and devotion to such worthy pursuits as farming, art collecting and music. Loyalty to king and country, domestic affection and stalwart Anglican faith were the virtues and values to which families such as the Austens of Steventon subscribed – though in their case, coupled with a lively sense of humour and, at times, an ironically irreverent outlook on life.

Even when announcing the arrival of his seventh child and second daughter, Jane, The Revd George Austen took a light-hearted tone. Writing a day later, on 17 December 1775, to his half-sister-in-law, Susanna Walter, he joked she had 'perhaps

············
**King George III**
Studio of Allan Ramsay, 1761–2
The dutiful, paternalistic king who helped sustain Britain's monarchy,
despite the loss of America and his eventual mental illness

**Sophia Charlotte of Mecklenburg-Strelitz**
Studio of Allan Ramsay, 1761–2
The much-loved wife of King George III,
and mother of fifteen children

wondered a little that we were in our old age grown such bad
reckoners', since his wife, Cassandra, had expected the baby a
month earlier. However, he reported cheerfully, 'We have now
another girl, a present plaything for her sister Cassy and a future
companion,' adding (with a sincere 'thank God') that Mrs
Austen was 'pure well'. Although Jane Austen's mother would
become increasingly hypochondriacal with age, demanding –
as Jane's letters would patiently show – constant attention for
ailments ranging from nervous headaches to 'Asthma, a Dropsy,
water in her Chest & a Liver Disorder', at a time when an
estimated one in seven women died in childbirth, she seemed
to survive the ordeal with little trouble, despite the 'violently

**Cassandra Austen**
Unknown artist, early
nineteenth century
Jane Austen's mother

rapid' rate at which she produced six sons and two daughters in
fourteen years. While her children were young she was evidently
an attentive and energetic mother, who not only gardened,
mended, oversaw the cooking and supervised the servants with
down-to-earth efficiency, but also ensured a lively atmosphere
for the household, encouraging games, jokes and fun of all
kinds – with an emphasis on wordplay, at which her younger
daughter especially excelled.

Both of Jane Austen's parents had an intellectual
background. Her mother – born Cassandra Leigh in 1739 –
was the daughter of a Fellow of All Souls, Oxford, and niece of
a Master of Balliol. Although, as a woman, she could not attend

a university herself or receive much formal education, she had what was described as a 'sprack [brisk] wit' and a talent for writing poetry, along with a love of reading, which made her well suited to become the wife, in 1764, of bookish young Oxford don and clergyman, George Austen. Socially, Mrs Austen was somewhat her husband's superior. A kinswoman of the titled Leigh family, owners of historic Stoneleigh Abbey in Warwickshire, she counted a duke among her maternal lineage, while the Austen forebears had been merely Kent clothiers, and George's father was a surgeon, then considered a relatively low-ranking profession. The death of both his parents when he was a child had, however, brought the young George under the care of a well-to-do uncle, Francis Austen, who paid for his education at Tonbridge School, and later at St John's College, Oxford, and remained his benefactor thereafter.

By the time Jane was born, her parents were comfortably settled. Not only had Uncle Francis provided a choice of two livings, or parishes, for her father, who had left Oxford for the Church, but another rich, land-owning relation, Thomas Knight, had presented him with a more profitable living as Rector of Steventon in Hampshire. There, in the rambling, old-fashioned rectory where she was born, Jane Austen would find the first outlets for her talent, in scribbling verses and stories to amuse her family. And there, in what her nephew and first full biographer, James Edward Austen-Leigh, would describe in his best-selling Memoir of 1870 as 'the cradle of her genius', she would, over her first, formative 25 years, acquire, develop and hone the extraordinary literary powers that would outlast her life and times, and reflect both her world and ours.

# The Austens at Home

'The Johnsons were a Family of Love; and though a little addicted to the Bottle and the Dice, had many good qualities' begins a passage in one of her hilarious childhood tales, 'Jack and Alice', and while the Austens were neither gamblers nor alcoholics, they were certainly a family of love. Of the eight Austen children, the eldest, James, born in 1765, had been followed in 1766 by George, who suffered from an unspecified disability that caused him to be brought up away from home and barely spoken of, although Mrs Austen once mentioned tenderly that her 'poor little George' had fits. Edward arrived in 1767, Henry in 1771, Cassandra in 1773, Francis in 1774 and finally, four years after Jane, in 1779, Charles – referred to fondly by his sisters as 'Our own particular little brother'.

Fiction is, of course, not autobiography. Both Jane's first biographers, her brother Henry and nephew James Edward, were at pains to stress that 'she drew from nature', not real life or individuals. She made the point herself, remarking on one occasion, 'I am too proud of my gentlemen to admit they were only Mr A. or Colonel B.', and noting after the publication of *Emma*, in 1815, that a friend was convinced she had based characters on acquaintances of hers: 'People whom I never heard of before.' Nonetheless, any novelist will inevitably be inspired and influenced to some degree by personal experience, and there would be much in her mature works that carried unmistakable echoes of her own childhood – in her first-sold, though last-published, novel, *Northanger Abbey* (1817), in particular. Like the realistically 'noisy and wild' heroine Catherine Morland, who grows up in a Georgian vicarage as one of a large, lively family, enjoying 'cricket, baseball, riding on horseback and running about the country', as well as 'rolling down the green slope at the back of the house', the young Austens grew up with a love of fresh air and outdoor activities; especially, in Jane's case, long country walks. 'We are desperate walkers!' she wrote on one occasion, evoking images of Lizzy Bennet in *Pride and Prejudice* 'crossing field after field at a quick pace, jumping over stiles and springing over puddles'. And it was surely no coincidence that at the back of Steventon Rectory there was a green, grassy slope.

## A 'Pleasant and Prosperous' Household

The rectory itself had little resemblance to the newly 'improved' houses in the elegant neoclassical style to which most of Jane Austen's female characters would aspire – let alone the grandeur of her great fictional mansions, such as Mr Darcy's Pemberley or the Bertrams' Mansfield Park. Demolished in the 1820s, by the Austens' day it was already considered decidedly outmoded, with exposed whitewashed beams and uncorniced ceilings, and simple furnishings, such as the chocolate-brown floral carpet and painted cupboard in the little sitting room off the bedroom that Jane shared with her sister Cassandra. It was also somewhat crowded, as The Revd George Austen took in boarding-pupils to help support his growing family. The income from the two Church livings was small and had frequently to be supplemented with loans from his rich relations. However, with the boarders' fees, as well as the profits and produce from a farm adjoining the rectory, Jane's father was able to keep a carriage and horses, employ a manservant, several maids and a cook,

...........
**Steventon Rectory**
Anna Austen, 1820s
Jane Austen's childhood home, drawn by her niece

and provide his wife and children with many of life's pleasures, from new clothes, holidays and a full social life to – most importantly – a ready supply of the latest books, as they came out.

The rising influence of radical ideas, such as those of the Geneva-born but French-settled writer Jean-Jacques Rousseau, then spreading throughout Europe, appeared to have little impact on the 'pleasant and prosperous' Steventon household.

Rousseau's belief that all mothers should breastfeed their own babies instead of consigning them to a wet nurse had led to a craze for the practice among fashionable Englishwomen. Mrs Austen apparently breastfed her babies briefly, but the infant Jane was soon 'put out to nurse' with a local villager in the traditional way and appeared to thrive on the process, developing into a healthy and highly intelligent child. One aspect of Rousseau's views on child-rearing that did, however, accord with those of the Austens was his belief that the young should be educated through play and self-expression rather than by strict rote. Jane evidently underwent the conventional early schooling described – with feeling – by Catherine Morland as 'poor little children first learning their letters and then learning to spell', equating 'to instruct' with 'to torment'; but the young Austens were also encouraged to develop their imaginations and explore words and ideas – even, at times, where Church matters were involved. Surviving Steventon parish records show that Jane was allowed to play around with the marriage entries, inserting her own name as the bride of invented grooms, ranging from 'Edmund Arthur William Mortimer of Liverpool' to plain 'Jack Smith'.

Scribbling in their schoolbooks was not frowned on either. Among several preserved by the family, a copy of the French primer *Fables Choisies* by Jean de La Fontaine, inscribed 'Jane Austen, Decr 5th 1783', contains the practice autographs 'Jane Austen' and 'Frank Austen' – as well as the striking words 'Mothers angry Fathers gone out' [sic]. Still more revealing are her forceful responses to the poet, novelist and playwright Oliver Goldsmith's popular *The History of England*: her copious pencil comments on his text are as entertaining as they are eloquent. At the age of twelve, Jane Austen was expressing opinions that

············
**Cassandra Austen**
John Miers, c.1809
Jane's beloved sister, to whom many
of her surviving letters are addressed

say much about her character, while showing a style and comic touch beyond her years. She is a rebel – vehemently dubbing King William III 'A Villain', and angered at the treatment of the Jacobites by the current Hanoverian King George III's antecedents – yet passionately pro-Royalist and, most significantly, anti-Republican. To Goldsmith's comment that Oliver Cromwell 'inherited a very small paternal fortune', she ripostes 'and that was more than he deserved'; while praise for the Parliamentarian John Hampden's good qualities elicits a stinging 'what a pity that such virtues shd be clouded by Republicanism!' According to her brother Henry's preface to *Northanger Abbey* and *Persuasion*, 'she seldom changed her opinions either on books or men', and already Jane Austen was showing every sign of the independent-minded woman and writer she was to become.

## 'A Little Education'

Although most of Jane Austen's education took place informally at home, when she was seven she was sent to a small boarding-school, located first in Oxford, then Southampton, run by a family connection of Mrs Austen's. It had been decided that her adored sister, Cassandra, should go, and since, as their mother put it, 'if Cassandra were going to have her head cut off,

............
OPPOSITE
**Oliver Goldsmith**
Studio of Joshua Reynolds, c.1770 or after
The playwright and author whose popular *The History of England* inspired
the young Jane Austen to write her own, hilarious, spoof 'History'

Jane would insist on sharing her fate', Jane went too. The experience was not happy. The proprietress proved dour and uncaring, and an epidemic of fever broke out, which both the Austen sisters caught. For Jane it was almost fatal, and although she recovered, it caused the death of another relation whose daughter was also a pupil. Despite this tragedy, they were later sent to another school, in Reading, presided over by one Mrs Latournelle. A kindly, if somewhat eccentric, widow with a false leg, she ran her establishment on free-and-easy lines resembling those of the fictional Mrs Goddard in *Emma*, to whose 'honest, old-fashioned boarding-school' girls were sent to 'scramble themselves into a little education without any danger of coming back prodigies'. It was a typically sly Jane Austen in-joke, for the benefit of her family and astute readers, that she named this imaginary headmistress of a little local girls' school after Dr Goddard, Headmaster of Winchester College, the famous boys' public school attended by her nephews.

## The 'Improvement of Her Mind'

Whether overtly or implicitly, women's education is an underlying theme in all Jane Austen's novels, from her caustic comment in *Northanger Abbey*, 'A woman, if she have the misfortune of knowing anything, should conceal it as well as she can', to Mr Darcy's rejoinder, when told the qualities required in an 'accomplished' woman: 'To all this, she must yet add something more substantial, in the improvement of her mind by extensive reading.' For all the exaggeration of Jane's self-deprecating claim, in a letter to the Prince Regent's unwitting librarian, in 1815, 'I think I may boast myself to be, with all possible vanity, the most unlearned and uninformed female who ever dared to be an authoress', she was certainly not brought up to be an intellectual prodigy. Under the traditional system deplored by her campaigning contemporary Mary Wollstonecraft, Latin and Greek, science and physics were for boys, to fit them for university and a paying career. Jane and Cassandra, as girls, would have studied only such subjects as scripture, geography and history, enough maths and book-keeping to equip them to run a household, and some French and Italian, along with the elegant female 'accomplishments' of drawing – at which Cassandra excelled – and music, for which Jane had a real talent. Although she professed a deep dislike of formal concerts and recitals – and particularly those amateurs who showed off limited skills in company – her nephew's *Memoir* recorded that she played the piano beautifully, and her surviving music books show a wide range of musical taste, from works by Handel and Haydn, and the English composers Thomas Arne and James Hook, to popular songs and ballads, such as 'Nobody Loves Like an Irishman'. But what mattered above all in the Austen family was 'extensive reading' – both for duty and pleasure. It was in her father's library of more than 500 books that Jane Austen's real education took place, and the foundations of her future career were laid.

## 'Extensive Reading'

Just as ingenuous young Catherine Morland discovers with enjoyment the works of Shakespeare, Pope and Gray, before being introduced to the contrasting delights of the latest horror fiction, from an early age Jane Austen devoured everything from 'history and belles lettres', classic prose and great poetry to the

............

LEFT
**George Crabbe**
William Holl Jr,
stipple engraving after
Thomas Phillips, 1847
The major Romantic poet,
whose works Jane admired so
much that she claimed she
would like to marry him

............

OPPOSITE
**Samuel Richardson**
Mason Chamberlin,
1754 or before
The author of the classic
epistolary novels *Pamela*
and *Clarissa*, as well as
Jane's lifelong favourite
*Sir Charles Grandison*

'mere Trash' of popular sentimental romances and the Gothic horror best-sellers that inspired *Northanger Abbey*. She read sermons and the essays of Joseph Addison and Richard Steele; and she relished all the classic English novels: Swift's *Gulliver's Travels*, Defoe's *Robinson Crusoe*, Fielding's *Tom Jones* and her lifelong favourite of all, Samuel Richardson's *The History of Sir Charles Grandison*. Although generally thought tedious today, *Grandison* was so beloved of Jane Austen that she spoke of the characters 'as if they had been living friends'. In poetry, her developing tastes ranged from the arch-Augustan Pope to the – for her, modern – Romantics: James Thomson, William Cowper and George Crabbe among them. In later years she would claim teasingly that she hoped to marry Crabbe and would look out for him while in London. However, according to her brother Henry, 'Her favourite moral writers were Johnson in prose and Cowper in verse'; and between the measured, enlightened sense of the one and lyrical sensibility of the other, perhaps no other authors did more to influence Jane Austen's literary development. Whether or not she made much use of Samuel Johnson's great *Dictionary of the English Language* (1755), given her tendency to spelling errors such as 'freindship' and 'veiw', she delighted in the classically balanced prose style, wit and erudition of 'my dear Dr Johnson', as she called him. She quoted him fondly, and would even pay his close companion Mrs Piozzi (the former Hester Thrale) the compliment of a Jane Austen parody, imitating her correspondence style in letters to Cassandra.

**Samuel Johnson**
James Barry, c.1778–80
The 'Great Lexicographer', essayist, critic, poet and novelist, whom Jane called 'my dear Dr Johnson'

## The Juvenilia

During the 1790s, Jane carefully copied out, at intervals, the mass of stories, verses, novellas and playlets that she had been writing since she was eleven or twelve years old. Amounting to some 74,000 words, the juvenilia are arranged, in no apparent order, into three large notebooks importantly entitled 'Volume the First', 'Volume the Second' and 'Volume the Third', as if they formed an actual three-volume novel. They contain signs of precocious wit and even genius in everything from the earliest fragments, such as 'Jack and Alice' and 'Henry and Eliza', to, as she matured, the longer, more ambitious first attempts at producing proper fiction, often in the novel-in-letters form then in vogue. While the childish pieces contain gems such as, 'The Door suddenly opened, and an aged gentleman … partly by intention and partly thro' weakness was at the feet of the lovely Charlotte' (from 'Frederic and Elfrida') and 'Alice had too sincere a respect for Lady Williams, and too great a relish for her Claret, not to make every concession in her power' (from 'Jack and Alice'), the later productions show the teenage Jane Austen beginning to explore real issues, notably regarding women and marriage. One, 'Catharine, or The Bower', involves a situation with special resonance in her family: the custom of sending young women of genteel birth but no financial prospects out to India, with the undisguised aim of finding husbands to provide for them from among the large population of single British men stationed there in the service of the governing East India Company.

# The Hastings Connection

Jane's aunt, The Revd George Austen's sister Philadelphia, had been one of those who joined the so-called 'fishing fleet'. Dispatched to Bengal 'for her maintenance', in 1752 she had duly married an East India Company surgeon twenty years her senior named Tysoe Saul Hancock, and in 1761 had borne a daughter, Elizabeth, whose baby nickname 'Betsy' gave way to 'Eliza'. Increasingly estranged from her staid, elderly husband, Philadelphia – who was beautiful and spirited – was well known to be a close friend of the first Governor-General of Bengal, the celebrated Warren Hastings, and according to rumour, Eliza, his god-daughter, was actually his child. The Austens possibly knew of the potential scandal: in a letter of 1813, Jane wrote elliptically, 'Mr Hastings never hinted at Eliza in the smallest degree'; but any such suspicions did nothing to detract from their affection for Eliza, or respect for Warren Hastings, with whom, through Philadelphia, they developed a warm acquaintance. Early in their marriage, Mr and Mrs Austen took Hastings's small son under their care at Steventon – English country air being thought healthier than the Indian climate. Tragically, the child died, but the bond between his father and Jane's family remained strong, and when, in 1788, a political storm erupted that saw Hastings impeached, charged with corruption, the Austens were among his staunch supporters.

..............

OPPOSITE
**Warren Hastings**
Sir Joshua Reynolds, 1766–8
Impeached for misconduct as Governor-General of Bengal, Hastings was eventually exonerated after the longest trial in British history. A friend of the Austens, he delighted Jane with his praise for *Pride and Prejudice*.

The seven-year trial in Westminster Hall – the longest
in British history – bitterly divided public and Establishment
opinion. Many (like Jane) regarded Hastings as a man of the
highest integrity: a fine and fair-minded colonial administrator,
who had sought to codify Hindu law, tackle famine relief and set
up a postal system, to the betterment of the native population.
Others, however, accused him of self-interest, malpractice and
financial profiteering, and their voices included some of the
most powerful and eloquent of the time: those of the great Whig
orators Charles James Fox and Edmund Burke, and the MP and
playwright Richard Brinsley Sheridan among them. Eventually,
Hastings was exonerated. Jane's brother Henry wrote him a
florid letter of congratulation, and the friendly connection
continued. In 1813, having sent him an early copy of *Pride and
Prejudice*, which he praised, Jane wrote to Cassandra, 'I am quite
delighted with what such a man writes about it.'

............

**For the Trial of Warren Hastings**
James Sayers, published February 1788
This cartoon by the caricaturist James Sayers
satirises the trial of Warren Hastings and features
some of its main protagonists: Edmund Burke,
Charles James Fox and Hastings himself.

## A New Influence

For the young Jane Austen, her cousin Eliza was a source
of fascinating insights into worlds beyond her own Hampshire-
parsonage upbringing. From exotic India, with its 'nabobs, gold
mohrs, and palanquins' (as airily cited in *Sense and Sensibility*),
George Austen's sister had taken her daughter to travel in
Europe, where during the 1770s she saw, at first hand, Queen
Marie-Antoinette holding court at Versailles, and in London
sampled the elegant life of the 'ton', the beau monde who set
the tone in fashionable dress, manners and tastes for Georgian
society. As a visitor to Steventon, pretty, coquettish Eliza caused
a considerable stir – something akin to the effect of seductive
Mary Crawford on the company at Mansfield Park. By the time
she became acquainted with the eleven-year-old Jane, in 1786,

**Eliza de Feuillide**
Unknown artist, c.1780
Jane and Cassandra's
fascinating, worldly-wise,
coquettish cousin, who
eventually married their
brother Henry in 1797

Eliza was already married, to a French army officer with the recently acquired title of Comte de Feuillide, and had a son, a sadly sickly child christened Hastings. Marriage and motherhood had, however, done nothing to quell her desire either for amusement or attention, especially from men, both of which – in the absence of her husband, who did not accompany her to England – she found at Steventon.

## Eliza and Entertainment

Along with reading aloud and reciting poetry, the young Austens loved acting. From about 1782, when Jane was aged seven, they put on plays, first in the family dining room, then in a barn converted for the purpose. Their choice of productions varied from tragedy to comedies, such as Sheridan's The Rivals, and the early eighteenth-century dramatist Susanna Centlivre's ironic The Wonder! A Woman Keeps a Secret; the players, besides the family themselves, included their father's pupils, local friends and neighbours, and any relations who might be staying. Another cousin, Philadelphia (or 'Phylly') Walter refused to join in, possibly because of scruples such as those of Fanny Price in Mansfield Park, about the impropriety of acting, since love scenes and physical contact might be involved. But Eliza was in her element on stage – taking lead roles and introducing into the repertoire fashionable plays that she had recently seen in resorts such as Tunbridge Wells. Despite being respectively four and ten years her junior, and despite her married status, Jane's eldest brother, James, and favourite brother, Henry, both fell for Eliza's flirtatious charms. And Jane, although never blind to vanity and

............
**Richard Brinsley Sheridan**
John Russell, 1788
The politician and playwright whose comedy
*The Rivals* the young Austens acted at Steventon

folly, and increasingly aware of her frivolous cousin's faults, was sufficiently fond of her to pay her a notable compliment: the manuscript of *Love and Freindship* bears the fulsome dedication: 'To Madame La Comtesse de Feuillide This Novel is inscribed by Her obliged Humble Servant The Author'.

The common twenty-first-century misconception that Jane Austen wrote 'heaving bosom' novels with constantly fainting heroines is instantly refuted by the merest glance at this masterpiece – in which she parodies literary silliness of every sort, but in particular, that of the sentimental-fiction genre familiar today as 'bodice-ripper' or 'Mills & Boon'. Alongside the classic popular novels of the age by major women writers such as Fanny Burney (Frances d'Arblay) and, later, Maria Edgeworth, the teenage Jane, her sister Cassandra and their friends revelled in badly written best-sellers filled with improbable happenings, forced coincidences and unnatural dialogue. *Love and Freindship* has everything from a fatal carriage accident (in the hero's 'fashionably high Phaeton') to larceny, elopement, rediscovered long-lost relations and two female friends of great beauty, self-proclaimed virtue and susceptibility to fainting fits. 'We fainted Alternately on a Sofa,' one of them writes impassionedly, and here the scope of Jane Austen's parody seems even to extend to the great Sheridan, whose *The Rivals* had recently been performed in the Steventon barn, and whose play *The Critic* includes the stage direction: 'They faint alternately in each other's arms.'

The growing confidence with which Jane Austen was writing as she approached adulthood is reflected in another minor masterpiece, dated 1791: her 'The History of England ... By a partial, prejudiced and ignorant Historian'. A skit on popular history in general, and Oliver Goldsmith's best-selling

account in particular, Jane's version revisits and elaborates
on the opinions she had earlier scribbled in the margins of his
book, expressing devotion to Charles l ('ever stedfast [sic] in
his own support') and Mary, Queen of Scots, 'This bewitching
Princess ... Abused, reproached & vilified by all.' Beneath
the fun, the work is skilfully crafted, and as much an astute
commentary on the dangers of received opinion and superficial,
unquestioned prejudice, as a mere send-up of a literary genre.

To accompany the text, Cassandra provided delightful
little watercolour illustrations of the various monarchs. Done
in witty caricature style, they were not intended as likenesses of
the actual historic characters but based on various Austen family
members in contemporary dress, their features and expressions
adapted to suit Jane's gleefully prejudiced attitudes. Mary, Queen
of Scots is, naturally, an image of saintly sweetness, and possibly
intended as a comically idealised portrait of Jane herself.

Miss
Godmer...
Fa...

... in a circumstance that any consultary which the Duchess
deems. — Butler has retired are to [?] raise advice,
are particular if well. — Sir Charles [?] with a genteel
little accident to [?] at [?] in hunting; he got off & had [?] here
over a hedge in a [?] in a [?], & his [?] is in [?]
less upon his leg, in rather awkward plight, & it is not [?]
whether he broke bone it or not he. — Howard [?] while is
a few miles from his cabbitt [?]; his friend [?] again
a little the other day, & Dr Littlefield has been [?], [?]
a little the other day. & D. Littlefield has been [?]
whether her accepts [?] invitation [?] [?] Richmond to [?]
he has not yet sent his own invitation, but that has

shi at
to the [?]
to him

Nov 1800

## Jane's Appearance

Jane Austen was not generally considered a beauty. In childhood, her cousin Phylly Walter described her, unkindly, as not only 'whimsical and affected' but also 'not at all pretty, & very prim, unlike a girl of twelve', whereas she thought Cassandra 'very pretty'. Recalling Jane as an adult, others were more complimentary, mentioning her bright hazel eyes, softly curling brown hair and fine – if somewhat high-coloured – complexion (hence perhaps the 'white & red' of Cassandra's famous portrait). 'Cheeks a little too full' was one slightly guarded comment from an otherwise approving observer. She was, however, slender, and tall for the time; in 1801, ordering herself a 'gown' (meaning dress material) of seven and a half yards, she noted 'it is for a tall woman'. Her brother Henry stated in his posthumous preface of 1817 that 'Her features were separately good', while praising her elegant 'carriage and deportment' and 'unrivalled expression'. If Cassandra was unquestionably 'the superior in beauty', as Jane would write of Marianne Dashwood in *Sense and Sensibility*, compared to her sister Elinor, Jane herself certainly grew into an attractive young woman, who loved clothes, gossip and parties (or 'balls', as even informal dances in private homes were termed), at which she rarely lacked for a partner.

..........
PREVIOUS PAGES
**Letter from Jane Austen to her sister Cassandra, 8–9 November 1800**
'To sit in idleness over a good fire in a well-proportioned room is a luxurious sensation ...'
One of the many letters that Jane sent to her sister, this example dates from the period between October 1800 and February 1801 when Cassandra was absent from home, visiting their brother Edward in Kent. The 25-year-old Jane provides news of domestic life (the purchase of new tables for the rectory and a storm that blew down trees in the garden) and the poor state of health of one of her admirers, Harris Bigg-Wither.

# Friends and Family

'Our neighbourhood was small, for it consisted only of your mother,' one letter in *Love and Freindship* begins equably, but fortunately for the convivial Austens, theirs was a far larger social circle. Among their many friends in the Hampshire area were the Digweed, Jervoise and Terry families; other intimates included the Bigg sisters, Catherine, Elizabeth and Alethea, at Manydown House, where the Austen girls often stayed, and Mrs Lefroy, the elegant, intelligent wife of the Rector of Ashe, whose company and conversation Jane, though much her junior, found delightful. But closest of all were Martha and Mary Lloyd, daughters of the clergyman's widow who rented George Austen's subsidiary living at Deane. Both of these young women were destined, both literally and figuratively, to become part of the Austen family.

The make-up of the Austen household changed considerably while Jane was growing up. Her eldest brother, James, and Henry, the brother to whom she was closest, went up to Oxford, to their father's old college, St John's. Aged about twelve, the younger Austen boys, Francis and Charles (who would eventually become admirals in the Royal Navy), went off to sea to begin training as midshipmen. And by 1783, when Jane was seven, her brother Edward (regarded, in the absence of the disabled George, as the second eldest) had left home permanently, to live with the Knights: the rich, childless son and daughter-in-law of Thomas Knight, who had provided The Revd George Austen with the Steventon living. They now made Edward their son and heir. Strange to modern sensibilities, such unofficial adoptions were not uncommon; in Jane's novels, they are the experience of both Fanny Price in *Mansfield Park*, and Frank Churchill in *Emma*. For Edward Austen, the outcome was a happy one. Now the heir to extensive property in Kent and Hampshire, he would in time become the owner of two great country houses with, as his main residence, Godmersham Park. He was sent on the Grand Tour, like other young men of rank, to take in the classical sights of Europe and hone his taste, and in 1791 he made an excellent marriage, to the beautiful daughter of a titled family, Elizabeth Bridges. A happy and well-suited couple, they would eventually have eleven children, of whom Fanny, the eldest, would become Jane's favourite niece. Although Edward's surname was changed to Austen-Knight – and later simply Knight – he remained close to his real family, who frequently stayed with him at Godmersham, amid what Jane wryly termed 'the Elegance & Ease & Luxury' of 'East Kent wealth'.

Her brother James's marriage, in 1792, brought Jane another sister-in-law – a general's daughter named Anne Mathew – and, a year later, her second niece, christened Jane Anna Elizabeth and known as Anna. But tragedy followed: in 1795, Anne died suddenly. And so when the alluring Eliza de Feuillide once again became a visitor to Steventon, James, as well as his bachelor brother Henry, was in a position to pay court to her – and this time with serious intent, for circumstances had changed dramatically. 'The politics of the day occupied very little of her attention,' James Edward Austen-Leigh would state in his *Memoir* of his aunt, and certainly there is no direct mention in any of Jane's writings of the outbreak of the French Revolution, in 1789, when she was thirteen. And the subsequent horror felt by herself and her family on learning, in 1794, that their own cousin Eliza's titled French husband had been one of the thousands who had gone to the guillotine can only be surmised. But whatever the immediate impact of that shock, it was to have a lasting effect on their family life. By the mid-1790s, Eliza was back in England, now a widow and apparently as determined as ever to enjoy life – and love.

James Austen had taken Holy Orders and become the incumbent of his father's secondary parish, at Deane. As a well-established widower with a small daughter, it seemed natural that he should now propose to the attractive widow with a small son, whom – in the discreet usage of the time – he had previously 'admired'. Eliza, however, refused him. She was once again enjoying her single status and its opportunities; and according to the Austen family tradition, just like worldly Mary Crawford in *Mansfield Park*, she had no desire to become the wife of a clergyman, with all the parish duties and personal restraints that would entail. It was perhaps in that knowledge that Henry Austen decided to forsake the Church as a career, and instead go into the militia, the auxiliary military force that, though part-time, not professional regular army, bestowed on its members all the cockaded, red-coated, sartorial glamour of regimentals, which even level-headed Lizzy Bennet in *Pride and Prejudice* would find enhanced any woman's 'first impressions' of a young man. Having also proposed to Eliza, and been turned down while he was destined for the Church, Henry asked her again, and in 1797 was accepted. James found consolation in another quarter: in the same year, he married Mary Lloyd, the younger of Jane and Cassandra's best friends.

## Dr Jenner and 'Mrs James'

The Lloyd girls – though 'sensible and good humoured' in Eliza's slightly condescending words – were not beauties, not least because they had both suffered from smallpox, which left them with pitted complexions. Smallpox remained a plague at this period, but medical advances were being made, largely through the introduction of vaccination. The early Georgian traveller Lady Mary Wortley Montagu, who had encountered the practice in Asia, had helped to make it fashionable, and King George III and Queen Charlotte – ever socially responsible – had endorsed it, having their children vaccinated. But the great pioneer was Dr Edward Jenner. His discovery that injecting a small quantity of cowpox into a human being could offer protection against smallpox was a breakthrough that he described in best-selling publications of 1798–1800. After an evening with friends in November 1800, Jane Austen reported that James and another guest had 'alternately read Dr Jenner's pamphlet on the cow pox'.

Its effect on his wife's looks did not diminish James's ardent feelings for her, however. A keen and accomplished poet, he wrote verses in his Mary's praise and, Jane noted with mounting irritation, seemed increasingly dominated by her. She complained that 'His Opinions' were 'too much copied from his Wife's', whom she came to find mean-spirited, humourless and – especially grating to her – uninterested in books of any sort. Jane was close to James's children, however, especially Anna, who did not get on well with her stepmother; and she would be remembered by James and Mary's son, her future biographer James Edward Austen-Leigh, in his Memoir as the

**Edward Jenner**
James Northcote, 1803
The medical pioneer responsible for the introduction of vaccination against smallpox.
In 1800, Jane mentioned her brother James reading 'Dr Jenner's pamphlet on the cow pox'.

most loyal and loving of aunts, an opinion shared by her many other nieces and nephews. 'She seemed to love you, and you loved her naturally in return,' one of them, James and Mary's daughter Caroline, later wrote – recalling stories, 'chiefly of Fairyland', with all the fairies being given different characters, and a delicious conversation with herself and other little girl cousins, 'supposing us grown up, the day after a Ball'.

············
**Thomas Langlois Lefroy**
George Engleheart, c.1799
Jane's first known admirer, with whom,
aged twenty, she danced and flirted. In a
distinguished legal career, he eventually
became Lord Chief Justice of Ireland.

# First Loves

The ideal, fulfilling love affair that would lead to marriage
and children of her own – assumed to be the inevitable goal
of all women at that time – was clearly much on Jane Austen's
mind, in both her real and imaginary worlds, during the 1790s.
The first of her surviving treasury of more than 160 letters, dating
from January 1796, when she was twenty, up until just weeks
before her death in 1817, focus, part-laughingly, part-excitedly,
on a flirtation she was then enjoying with a nephew of her friend
Mrs Lefroy, named Thomas Lefroy. Tom, who was Irish, was just
twenty years old: 'a very gentlemanlike, pleasant, good-looking
young man' in Jane's words. The attraction between them clearly
caused some comment among those who saw them together,
bringing a mild reproof from the ever-correct Cassandra. 'You
scold me so much,' Jane responded mischievously the day after
a local dance, 'that I am almost afraid to tell you how my Irish
friend and I behaved. Imagine to yourself everything most
profligate and shocking in the way of dancing and sitting
down together.'

As though picturing her situation in a novel, she tried
out various dramatic possibilities – declaring at one point that
she was expecting a marriage proposal from him, yet in the
same letter dismissing him, with the air of a seasoned flirt, as
'Mr. Tom Lefroy, for whom I do not care sixpence'. And on his
departure soon after, to return to Ireland, where he would forge
a distinguished legal career, rising eventually to become Lord
Chief Justice, she cast herself delightedly in the role of a stock
heroine in a sentimental novel-in-letters, reporting on a doomed
love: 'The Day is come on which I am to flirt my last with Tom

Lefroy .... My tears flow as I write, at the melancholy idea.'
Whatever actually passed between the couple, the person who
knew Jane best, Cassandra, clearly did not think it of any deep
importance, since the references were left for posterity, when,
after her sister's death, she undertook the destruction of many
passages – and evidently whole letters – relating to intimate
feelings and events.

There was, however, a literary legacy from the affair. It was
about this time, according to notes made by Cassandra, that Jane
Austen was at work on a novel-in-letters entitled 'Elinor and
Marianne': an early draft version of the novel that, much revised,
would later be known to the world as *Sense and Sensibility*. Not
only does it include a serious-minded elder sister trying to check
a younger from displaying too openly her feelings for a handsome
admirer; it also shows the unguarded young couple, in the first
throes of attraction, comparing their tastes in reading. For
ardent Marianne Dashwood, this means discovering a mutual
passion for the Romantics, Cowper especially; Jane Austen and
Tom Lefroy daringly discussed Fielding's bawdy novel *Tom Jones*.
It was, Jane decided, in honour of Tom Jones, who wore a white
coat, that Tom Lefroy had a morning coat in the same, by then
unfashionable, colour. 'I shall refuse him,' she wrote mirthfully,
'unless he promises to give away his white coat.'

Strikingly, there is a gap in the letters for the year 1797.
Presumably, when editing them after Jane's death, Cassandra
chose to excise all mention of the tragedy unfolding in her own
life at that time. She had become engaged to Thomas Fowle,
a former pupil of George Austen's. Saving for their future,
Tom Fowle, having taken orders, had gone to serve as an army
chaplain in the West Indies: while there, he fell victim to the

...........
**Henry Fielding**
After William Hogarth,
after 1762
In 1796, Jane daringly
discussed Fielding's
bawdy novel *Tom Jones*
with her admirer,
Thomas Lefroy

plague of yellow fever, and died, leaving Cassandra endowed
with his worldly goods, worth £1,000, but emotionally bereft.
She, like Jane, would never marry – despite some occasional
matchmaking attempts, worthy of Emma Woodhouse in
*Emma*, on the part of her family.

Another tentative romance for Jane, in 1798, also came
to nothing. Again, her admirer – a clergyman and Fellow of
Emmanuel College, Cambridge, named The Revd Samuel

Blackall – was staying with Mrs Lefroy at Ashe when he and Jane were introduced; perhaps this fond older friend was also trying some discreet matchmaking. Again, however, there would be no great love affair, although the young people clearly made a lasting impression on one another. In a letter to Mrs Lefroy, Blackall wrote cautiously that he would like to become better acquainted with the Austen family, 'with a hope of creating to myself a nearer interest. But at present I cannot indulge any expectation of it.' Jane's response, on being shown the letter, was as level-headed as ever: 'It will all go on exceedingly well, and decline away in a very reasonable manner.' But in 1813, hearing of his marriage, she wrote affectionately: 'He was a piece of Perfection, noisy Perfection himself which I always recollect with regard.' Inevitably, she proceeded to invent a character for his wife, imagining her as 'rather ignorant, but naturally intelligent ... fond of cold veal pies, green tea in the afternoon, & a green window blind at night'.

## Literary Developments

The observation, wit and imagination that Jane brought to bear on every aspect of her real life was at the same time being channelled, to increasingly brilliant effect, into her fiction. According to notes made by Cassandra as to the chronology of her sister's composition, it was in 1796 that Jane began work on 'First Impressions', the novel that would eventually become *Pride and Prejudice*, and she completed it in August 1797. The book was an instant success with its first readers – her family and friends. 'I would not let Martha read 'First Impressions' again on any account,' Jane wrote laughingly to Cassandra in 1799: 'she means to publish it from memory, and one more perusal must enable her to do it.' In fact, publication of 'First Impressions' had by then already been attempted. In November 1797, Jane's father contacted the London publishing firm of Cadell, informing them that he had in his possession 'a Manuscript Novel, comprised in 3 Vols, about the length of Miss Burney's Evelina' and enquiring if they would like to see it. The response was disheartening. By return of post, Cadell summarily turned down, sight unseen, the offer of the future *Pride and Prejudice*. It was one of the great publishing rejections of history.

Its 'authoress' seemed, however, undaunted by the disappointment. Her day-to-day existence continued as before, with all its agreeable occupations of writing, dancing, reading, family affairs and visits to friends. It was while she was away from home, in November 1800, staying with her and Cassandra's beloved friend Martha Lloyd, that a decision was made in her absence that would end, abruptly, this happy and productive first phase of her life. Her father, now aged seventy, decided to retire and hand over their Steventon home and living to his eldest son, James. As Jane entered the door on her return, accompanied by Martha, Mrs Austen greeted her excitedly with the words, 'Well girls, it is all settled! We have decided to leave Steventon and go to Bath.'

At this, according to family tradition, Jane fainted.

# 'FRESH SCENES AND NEW ACQUAINTANCE'

'God made the country, and man made the town.'
William Cowper, The Task, 1785

'Another stupid party last night.'
Jane Austen, letter from Bath, 1801

When the first shock of learning that she was to leave
Steventon, the home she loved, and go to live in Bath, a place she
disliked, had subsided, Jane responded to the situation with her
customary good sense and self-command. 'I get more & more
reconciled to the idea of our removal. We have lived long enough
in this Neighbourhood,' she wrote in January 1801, adding
resolutely: 'There is something interesting in the bustle of going
away, & the prospect of spending future summers by the Sea or
in Wales is very delightful.' She kept herself, and her thoughts,
determinedly occupied with the practical business of packing up
the rectory and helping to dispose of the contents – though with
mixed success. Recording the prices achieved for the furniture
a few months later, she mentioned 'the blow of only Eleven
Guineas for the Tables', but some of her books did well: 'Ten
shillings for Dodsley's Poems however please me to the quick,'

............
OPPOSITE
**King's Circus, Bath**
One of the many elegant developments in the city designed
by the eminent architect John Wood the Elder in the 1720s

she noted with satisfaction. Money, as she was well aware, would be a matter of increasing concern in her life from now on.

Beneath the determined cheerfulness, however, there could be little doubt as to her real feelings. A loyal 'Hampshire-born Austen', as she called herself, like all her fictional heroines Jane was by instinct and upbringing a dedicated countrywoman – revelling in what she called 'the exquisite enjoyment of air', the pace and freedom of rural life and, above all, the beauties of landscape. She took pleasure in occasional town visits, to London, especially, for the shopping and variety of social activities to be found there. But the deep unhappiness of Anne Elliot, heroine of her last-completed novel, *Persuasion*, on being obliged by family pressure to leave her happy country-childhood surroundings to reside full time amid the 'vapour, shadow, smoke, and confusion' of the once-fashionable West Country watering-place undoubtedly reflected her own feelings.

## Bath Beginnings

The city was already past its early eighteenth-century heyday when Jane first went there, in the 1790s, on holiday. Once a thriving Roman resort known as Aquae Sulis, where people met to bathe in the hot mineral waters that welled up from the surrounding limestone, Bath had, by Georgian times, fallen from favour as a venue for well-to-do visitors. But in the early 1700s, an ambitious Welsh-born entrepreneur named Richard Nash saw its potential to become, once again, a popular (and highly commercial) spa town. He persuaded Bath Corporation to appoint him official master of ceremonies,

..........
**Richard ('Beau') Nash**
After William Hoare, c.1761
The entrepreneur who in
the early 1700s oversaw the
transformation of Bath into
an elegant, well-run and
architecturally outstanding
centre of fashionable
entertainment

and over the next decades, with the backing of businessmen
and planners, 'Beau' Nash, the self-styled 'King of Bath',
oversaw a historic transformation. A new Pump Room was
built, where visitors could meet to take the warm, healing
waters; the latest developments in urban amenities, from broad
pavements to good street lighting, were introduced; a strict code
of manners was enforced; and a social routine of regular, formal
public engagements, from concerts to balls, was established.
A visitors' book prominently placed in the Pump Room recorded
the names and addresses of all the latest arrivals, enabling the
temporary residents to pay the all-important formal duty 'calls'
on one another.

The wealthy flocked to see and be seen in Bath; to meet friends and acquaintances, and – importantly, in many cases – make new ones. With an official master of ceremonies in charge of proceedings at the balls in the newly built Upper and Lower Assembly Rooms, entrusted with introducing those present to one another, Bath became a place where the eligible unattached might meet not only dancing partners but also potential marriage partners. It is in this way, at a ball in the Lower Assembly Rooms, that the heroine of *Northanger Abbey*, Catherine Morland, first meets the hero, Henry Tilney; although by the time their fictional encounter takes place (as Jane Austen stresses in her preface to this novel, conceived in the 1790s), times, and Bath life, had changed. Beau Nash had been succeeded by new masters of ceremonies, among them the Mr King of the novel, and the older generation – such as, in fiction, Henry Tilney's father and Catherine Morland's chaperone, and, in real life, Jane Austen's parents – were becoming the mainstay of the city's population. The young and fashionable were to be found now in newer, livelier settings, such as Cheltenham – and the seaside resort of Brighton, where the Prince of Wales's (and future Prince Regent's) exotic holiday home, the Royal Pavilion, was taking ever more elaborate and expensive shape. To 'elegant' young Emma Woodhouse in *Emma*, written in 1815, it is almost an insult when social upstart Mrs Elton attempts to persuade her to visit Bath, under the aegis of a friend of hers there: 'some vulgar, dashing widow', Emma angrily surmises.

# Architecture and Addresses

Even the glorious architecture for which Bath is today
internationally renowned, apparently held little charm for
Jane Austen, who wrote with dislike of 'the white glare' of the
stonework. In the 1720s, the architect John Wood the Elder
began to lay out the city on classical lines – inspired in part by
its setting, like that of Rome itself, among seven hills. Built in
pearly white local stone – since mellowed to a warm honey-gold
– the orderly squares and crescents of Bath presented a vista of
austere, geometrically planned yet harmonious beauty, with all
the light and elegance of vast windows and lofty rooms within.
Queen Square, famously, was designed to look like the palatial
frontage of a great pillared and pedimented mansion with wings.
In 1799, on another family visit, when her rich brother Edward
went to take the waters, Jane lodged at no. 13 and on this
occasion was 'exceedingly pleased' with her surroundings,
praising the comfort and the 'nice-sized rooms'. With shifting
tastes, however, fashions in addresses (as in so much else)
changed: writing the second of her great Bath novels, *Persuasion*,
Jane Austen has a young female character say firmly: 'We must
be in a good address. ... None of your Queen Squares for us.'
Every address given to the characters in that novel is chosen
with artful care, as a subtle indicator both of status and
aspirations – from snobbish Sir Walter Elliot's residence in
'lofty, dignified' Camden Place, to the impoverished, worthy

............
OVERLEAF
**The Circus from 'Eight Views of the most Elegant Scenes of and in Bath'**
John Robert Cozens, published 1773
A contemporary etching with watercolour that depicts the work of the
architect John Wood the Elder.

widow Mrs Smith's wrong-end-of-town lodgings in humble Westgate Buildings.

As a visitor, while still relatively young, Jane – like Catherine Morland – had found plenty to enjoy in the 'variety of amusements' on offer. Along with the 'regular duties' of drinking glasses of the health-giving waters, inspecting the visitors' book and promenading around the Pump Room, 'quizzing' (or eyeing) the company to the sound of 'a good band of musick', there were local delicacies to be tasted, such as Bath Oliver biscuits, named after famous local physician William Oliver, and the pastries known as 'Sally Lunns' (or 'Bath Bunns', as Jane jokingly misspelt them). There was the theatre to be attended and, not least, the weekly Assembly Room balls to look forward to. As a reluctant full-time resident in her early thirties, however, despite what her nephew's 1870 *Memoir* would term 'Fresh scenes and new acquaintance', Jane would find little to fulfil her in the city's physical and social confinement, and crowded, noisy surroundings.

## A Family Scandal

Finding a new home in Bath in 1801 proved far from easy. To begin with the Austens lodged with Mrs Austen's rich, childless sister, Mrs Leigh-Perrot, and her husband, James, who lived for part of the year in an elegant house at No. 1, Paragon Buildings. Shockingly, their hostess, an odd and difficult woman, had not long before been charged with shoplifting. While awaiting trial, she had spent time in prison, lodged with a warder, where Mrs Austen had somewhat startlingly suggested

Jane and Cassandra should join her to be of comfort and help. That offer, fortunately, was declined, and Mrs Leigh-Perrot was eventually found innocent, apparently a victim of blackmail, but her eccentric company can have done little to lift Jane's already lowered spirits.

The house the Austens finally settled on – to Jane's relief – was in Sydney Place, which at least afforded a view of the green, airy space and trees of Sydney Gardens, a pleasure-garden and popular setting for concerts and walks: 'We can go into the Labyrinth every day,' she wrote with somewhat forced jauntiness. The tone of her letters remained determinedly positive as she sent and received news of her brothers' fortunes at sea, the health of her mother and the progress of her much-loved nieces and nephews. Yet there was evidently little real pleasure for her in Bath life, with its round of tedious card parties, sedate walks with her uncle to drink the medicinal waters and formal calls on dull acquaintances. 'Another stupid party last night,' she wrote jadedly on 12 May 1801. Even the regular Assembly Rooms balls now proved a disappointment: 'There was only one dance, danced by four couple,' she reported after one ball, in the Upper Rooms. 'It was shockingly and inhumanly thin for this place.'

As if to keep her spirits up with a subject always close to her heart, Jane became more preoccupied than ever with dress and fashion. One of the few genuine pleasures she could still find in Bath was shopping, and she wrote constantly of her latest purchases, describing her choices of fabrics and colours and the successes, or failures, of her dressmakers. While accessories such as bonnets, gloves and shawls could be bought ready-made, dresses had to be made entirely by hand. Buying gowns –

as Henry Tilney does for his sister in *Northanger Abbey* – meant the purchase of dress-lengths of material, to be made up according to the wearer's size and specifications. Much of a letter dated 5 May 1801 to her equally fashion-conscious sister, Cassandra, is taken up by a minute description of a new 'round gown' she is having made by a Mrs Mussell, including even a sketched detail of the bodice back. She does not, on this occasion, specify the actual colour or fabric of the dress – and the choice in the Bath shops was wide, from soft muslins and cambrics to fine silks, in every shade from subtle brown to the flashy red 'coquelicot' favoured by Catherine Morland's showy friend Isabella Thorpe. Most stylish of all at this period, however, was the simple white muslin gown: the deceptively understated yet flattering choice of the truly elegant and well-bred woman. 'Put on a white gown; Miss Tilney always wears white' is one of the rare pieces of worthwhile advice Catherine Morland receives from her clothes-mad chaperone.

## Modes and Manners

'Dress is at all times a frivolous distinction,' Jane writes with mock severity in *Northanger Abbey*, as if warding off critics and moralists, as Catherine Morland lies awake the night before an Assembly Rooms ball, debating between 'her spotted and her tamboured muslin' gowns. But, to the author and her Regency readers, dress was in reality a matter of consuming importance. Even her most virtuous and high-minded heroine, Fanny Price in *Mansfield Park*, faced with the question of 'how she should be dressed' for her first ball, is soon deep in 'the interesting

**Beau Brummell**
John Cook, after an
unknown miniaturist,
published by Richard
Bentley, 1844
The ultimate dandy,
and arbiter of Regency
modes and manners

subject'. In fashion, as in all aspects of taste, Jane Austen – like
most of her contemporaries – inevitably reflected the influence
of the great arbiter of modes and manners, George 'Beau'
Brummell, even if it was not necessarily a connection she herself
would have recognised. Close friend of the Prince of Wales,
lionised habitué of aristocratic London circles and source of
edicts such as, 'If John Bull [the man in the street] turns around
to look after you, you are not well-dressed', Brummell moved
in very different social circles from Jane's, and these two great
figures of the age assuredly never met. But the aesthetic climate

in which Jane Austen lived and wrote, and the standards of appearance and behaviour by which she expected her fictional characters to be judged, were those of Brummell and the austerely elegant dandy ethos that, if he did not single-handedly introduce, he certainly codified and established.

As a true dandy – the antithesis of a fop – Brummell advocated simplicity and understatement, immaculate attention to detail and, above all, a disdain for pretentiousness or show – as Jane did in her ideas and writing. He persuaded the vain, extravagant Prince of Wales (and hence the rest of British male society) to abandon such fopperies as lavish satin waistcoats with elaborate jewelled buttons in favour of simple dark clothes, perfectly cut and tailored from fine cloth, relying for impact on fit, not ostentation. The other extreme of affectation in men's dress – the pose of deliberate slovenliness, adopted by the Whig leader Charles James Fox, among others, to show radical ideals and disdain for social convention – was equally abhorrent to Brummell, whose insistence on freshly washed under-linen and finely starched cravats was legendary.

## Romance and Radicalism

Understatement now ruled women's dress, too. Worn low cut and clinging, in a look reminiscent of classical statuary, the simple white muslin gown could be the height of expensive elegance, yet the colour and fabric were also expressive of the love of nature and disregard for finery associated with the Romantic ideal. It was in a soft, unadorned and apparently uncorseted white gown that the great feminist Mary Wollstonecraft sat for

............
**Charles James Fox**
Karl Anton Hickel, 1794
The Whig party leader, Fox cultivated a slovenly
appearance and demeanour, in keeping with
his radical disdain for convention.

her portrait, shortly before her tragic death giving birth to the future Mary Shelley, author of Frankenstein, in 1797.

Mary Wollstonecraft's impact on the public was sensational. A republican and passionate supporter of the ideals of the American and French revolutions, she fearlessly attacked the conventions and institutions of eighteenth-century society, proclaiming not only the rights of man, but also of woman. Part of the political and intellectual circle that included Tom Paine – whose revolutionary activities led to him being accused of treason – she achieved international fame with her two most famous works, A Vindication of the Rights of Men and A Vindication of the Rights of Woman. Published in 1790 and 1792 respectively, they both became best-sellers, and with her wide-ranging literary tastes, the young Jane Austen unquestionably knew them.

Many aspects of their author's life and thinking were entirely contrary to her own. The British public were shocked when, in 1798, Mary's husband and fellow-Romantic, William Godwin, published a loving biography of his late wife, which revealed what many considered scandalous facts. She had lived with a man outside marriage and had an illegitimate child; worse still, to contemporary opinion, she had attempted suicide, then not merely a sin but a crime. The bachelor novelist Horace Walpole dubbed her a hyena in petticoats'; his friend the educationalist and evangelical Hannah More, authoress of works of an improving nature, assured him that she had not read the Vindication, protesting: 'There is something fantastic and absurd

............
OPPOSITE
**Mary Wollstonecraft**
John Opie, c.1797
The pioneering feminist and writer

............
LEFT
**William Godwin**
James Northcote, 1802
Husband of Mary Wollestonecraft
and author of a loving *Memoir* of
his wife, which inadvertently
damaged her reputation

............
OPPOSITE
**Hannah More**
Henry William Pickersgill, 1822
Writer, educationalist and
evangelist, whose most popular
work Jane suspected of 'pedantry
and affectation'

in the very title.' Questions of personal morality and even anti-
monarchist, republican political attitudes aside, Jane Austen
(who joked about some of Hannah More's books) had one very
good reason for distancing herself, in print, from their radical
fellow-writer: Mary Wollstonecraft strongly believed that reading
novels was bad for women and should be avoided. And this was
an argument that, to Jane, required refuting.

While living in Bath, in 1803, Jane had another attempt
at getting her work published, and this time came close to
success. A bookseller, Crosby & Co., paid £10 for the manuscript
of 'Susan', a novel she had begun to write in 1798 or 1799.
Frustratingly, though advertised, it was not published, and
would not appear until 1817, reworked and retitled as *Northanger*

*Abbey*. By that time, Jane explained in a preface to the work, written shortly before her death, 'places, manners, books and opinions' had changed greatly. One of her own opinions remained unaltered, however: the merits, as well as pleasure, of 'a good novel' and the need for intelligent readers to come to its defence against those who would dismiss it as a trifling and unworthy art-form, with the well-known words, 'Oh it is only

a novel'. With demure yet forceful wit, in a famous passage from *Northanger Abbey*, Jane singles out especially other fiction-writers who profess to condemn novels, while producing them themselves. A reference to Mary Wollstonecraft, author of two well-known and well-regarded novels, seems likely here; further underlined by Jane's tongue-in-cheek invocation of the importance of solidarity among heroines on the subject. 'Let us leave it to the reviewers to abuse such effusions of fancy,' she teases; 'Let us not desert one another; we are an injured body.'

Yet on a greater scale, Jane Austen and Mary Wollstonecraft were united in their beliefs about oppression, injustice and exploitation of all kinds, and of their own sex in particular. Jane, unlike Mary, does not seek to unpick the stitches that bind society. She never voices a direct attack on the limitations of women's education; she deplores sexual licence, and she believes in the institution of marriage – though if, and only if, based on genuine, mutual love and respect: 'Oh Lizzy! do anything rather than marry without affection,' Jane Bennet implores her sister in *Pride and Prejudice*, and Jane Austen, speaking from the heart, uses almost the same forceful phrase to her beloved niece Fanny Knight, urging: 'Anything is to be preferred or endured, rather than marrying without Affection.' Her fervent belief in women's ultimate right to self-determination is voiced simply but surely in the declaration by Elizabeth Bennet, her favourite heroine: 'I am only resolved to act in that manner which will, in my own opinion, constitute my happiness.'

## Love and Loss

Two last marriage opportunities for Jane came to nothing. In 1802, while she and Cassandra were staying with their friends the Bigg sisters at Manydown House, she received – and accepted – an offer of marriage from their brother, Harris Bigg-Wither. But he was six years her junior and, more importantly, she did not love him. Overnight she changed her mind, and she and Cassandra left the house precipitately the next morning. Another apparently serious marriage possibility ended in tragedy. According to Cassandra, while staying at a seaside resort, Jane met an unnamed man to whom she was deeply attracted, as he was to her – feelings that Cassandra believed would have led to marriage. But not long after, they received word that this man had died. Jane was by then in her late thirties; her future role would be that of dependent daughter and much-loved aunt.

The death of The Revd George Austen in January 1805 left 'our dear Trio', as Henry Austen called his mother and sisters, with an annual income of barely £210 between them. 'Single women,' as Jane would write later to her niece Fanny, 'have a dreadful propensity for being poor.' Her hopes of making money from her writing seemed as unlikely as ever to be fulfilled. 'Susan' remained unpublished, and a new novel, entitled 'The Watsons', which she began in Bath, was left unfinished after some 17,500 words had been written. The Austen brothers came to their aid, topping up their income with contributions, and they moved house to smaller lodgings in Gay Street, where only one maid was required, and then to Trim Street. But in June 1806, to Jane's overwhelming relief, they left Bath for good – 'With what happy feelings of Escape!' she later wrote.

## Life Beyond Bath

After a stay in Clifton, on the outskirts of Bristol, and some family visits, a happier phase began in Jane's life with another move, to Southampton, where, with her brother Frank and his new wife (another Mary), the Austen women set up home in Castle Square. Jane's letters show now a renewed delight in some of her greatest pleasures: gardening, poetry and the navy. 'I could not do without a syringa,' she wrote, 'for the sake of Cowper's Line,' a reference to the poet's words: 'Laburnum, rich/In streaming gold; syringa, iv'ry pure', from *The Task*. She was living near the sea again, which she loved. Holidays in the seaside resorts of Sidmouth and Lyme Regis, where she could indulge in sea-bathing, had been her great solace during the Bath sojourn. Above all, she had once again the company of Frank: the epitome of the warm-hearted, practical, sensible naval officer who – even more than the dandyish, if desirable, Mr Darcy, with his cool put-downs – was clearly her masculine ideal in life and in fiction. Frank, many believed, would be the model for Captain Wentworth, hero of *Persuasion*.

The statement of James Edward Austen-Leigh in his *Memoir* that politics interested his aunt very little was perhaps borne out by Jane Austen's surviving comments on her naval brothers and their careers. She was fascinated by their lives and experiences. She read the Navy Lists, wrote excitedly of their promotions and changes of ship, and was continually concerned for their welfare. Having sought their permission, she used names of their actual ships in her fiction, and she prided herself on knowing a sloop from a frigate. Yet little of the bigger picture of the long-drawn-out war at sea against Napoleonic France,

..........
**William Cowper**
George Romney, 1792
The leading Romantic poet was a favourite of Jane Austen –
and of the fictional Marianne Dashwood in *Sense and Sensibility*.

············
**Horatio Nelson**
Sir William Beechey, 1800
Commander-in-Chief of the Royal Navy,
in which Jane Austen's brothers Francis and
Charles served with distinction. Nelson's
heroic death at the Battle of Trafalgar in
1805 caused a national outpouring of grief.

············
**Sir John Moore**
Thomas Lawrence, c.1800–4
Moore's famous victory over the
French at the Battle of Corunna
in 1809, later immortalised in
poetry, was mentioned by Jane
in her letters.

in which Frank and Charles were engaged for much of her adult
life, emerges directly from her writings. The crucial Battle of
Trafalgar in 1805 (like the Battle of Waterloo, a decade later) does
not feature in her letters or fiction, except as a fleeting reference
to house and street names in 'Sanditon'. And the nation's hero,
Admiral Lord Nelson, is mentioned only when she writes
flippantly of Robert Southey's biography of him in 1813: 'I am
tired of Lives of Nelson, being that I never read any. I will read
this, though, if Frank is mentioned in it.'

The death of General Sir John Moore at Corunna in 1809 is referred to by Jane Austen in her letters, yet her comments largely concern his dying words and his mother's likely feelings. She was entirely abreast of the tumultuous events unfolding in the world: she read the newspapers, peopled her novels with naval men and occasional soldiers, and read books such as Captain C.W. Pasley of the Royal Engineers' critique on Britain's military policy in the war against Napoleon – a work that, as a devout patriot, she expected to dislike, but instead found 'delightfully written', calling the author 'the first soldier I ever sighed for'. Her overriding interest was in the personal and the human. As she perceptively remarked herself, after visiting a museum and a gallery in London in 1811: 'My preference for Men & Women, always inclines me to attend more to the company than the sight.'

The pleasant life in Southampton was tragically interrupted when, in 1808, her brother Edward's wife Elizabeth died after giving birth to her eleventh child. While Cassandra, who was at Godmersham, remained there to care for the other children, Jane had the two eldest boys, Edward and George, aged fourteen and twelve, to stay with her. She looked after them with insight and tact – encouraging them to shed tears if they wished, but mainly cheering them up with diversions, from books to 'spillikins, paper ships, riddles, conundrums and cards'. Edward's gratitude to his sisters took a welcome form: he offered them, from among his properties, a new home. After some initial thoughts of Kent, a small house close to his manor at Chawton was settled on. And so, in the summer of 1809, Jane Austen, her mother, her sister Cassandra and their indispensable friend Martha Lloyd moved back to Hampshire, to the unassuming brick-built cottage that is today a place of literary pilgrimage.

# SENSE

### AND

# SENSIBILITY:

## A NOVEL.

### IN THREE VOLUMES.

## BY A LADY.

### VOL. I.

### London:

PRINTED FOR THE AUTHOR,

By C. Roworth, Bell-yard, Temple-bar,

AND PUBLISHED BY T. EGERTON, WHITEHALL.

1811.

# 'HER CAREER AS A WRITER'

'Mr Murray's letter is come. He is a rogue
of course, but a civil one.'
Jane Austen, letter from London, 1815

'Pray, dear Madam, soon write again and again.'
Letter to Jane Austen from The Revd J.S. Clarke,
Librarian to the Prince Regent, 1815

The first of Jane Austen's novels to be published, *Sense and Sensibility*, centres on a widow and her dependent daughters, who go to live, on a reduced income, in a cottage belonging to a rich relation. And, in 1809, Mrs Austen and her unmarried daughters moved into the cottage at Chawton that her landowner son Edward Austen-Knight had provided for them, close to one of the great houses he had inherited from his adoptive parents. Despite having six bedrooms, Chawton Cottage was far from elegant: formerly a bailiff's lodging, it overlooked a busy main road, where carts, carriages and mail coaches rumbled or raced by continually, and a nearby pond regularly flooded, causing one small niece to call it 'the pondy house'. Nevertheless, to Jane it represented, at last, the settled home, in her beloved Hampshire, she longed for.

Our Chawton home, how much we find
Already in it, to our mind;
And how convinced, that when complete,
It will all other Houses beat

So Jane wrote jauntily in a verse-letter to her brother
Frank in July 1809. A few minor improvements were made by
Edward to give the family more privacy. A front window was
blocked up – allowing an all-important bookcase to be installed
behind it – and a new entrance at the side was created, giving on
to the garden, which contained a tree-lined shrubbery walk and
an orchard. Passers-by could still see Mrs Austen gardening in
a green smock, and even seated at breakfast, in one of the two
parlours opening off the little central hall. But despite the
constant bustle, interruptions and demands of family, visitors
and housekeeping business, Jane now found herself able to
focus on her long-held ambition: not merely to write again,
but to become, at last, a published author.

Her first step towards the goal was to reassess the existing
manuscripts she had kept since Steventon days. 'Susan', the
future *Northanger Abbey*, remained unpublished, and 'First
Impressions', the future *Pride and Prejudice*, had already suffered
a disappointing rejection twelve years earlier. And so it was the
work initially drafted as a novel-in-letters, under the title 'Elinor
and Marianne', that Jane Austen now chose to revive and rework,
sitting at a little mahogany table in the Chawton dining room.
According to family tradition, the room had a creaking door,
which she refused to have silenced, since it gave her warning
when her work was about to be interrupted.

With *Sense and Sensibility*, not only would the situation of

............
**Chawton Cottage, Hampshire**
'Our Chawton home', where Jane Austen lived
from 1809 until just before her death in 1817

the main characters as financially dependent women reflect an immediate concern of Jane's, but through its plot and central themes she was also able to explore a social and artistic debate of profound interest to her: the conflict between 'sense' (or reason) and 'sensibility' (or unrestrained, even self-indulgent, displays of feeling). Hot-headed Marianne Dashwood, the archetypal teenage rebel, in giving free rein to a warm heart and youthful disdain for social convention puts not only her own, but also others', happiness at risk. Although her sister Elinor is willing to accept and observe the social proprieties, to the extent of 'telling lies when politeness required it', she is – Jane Austen makes clear – a no less sensitive and loving individual. However, she is a more admirable one. 'Her feelings were strong, but she knew how to govern them' is the author's telling phrase.

............

**William Gilpin**
Henry Walton, 1781
Author of a best-selling series of works on the appreciation of
'Picturesque' scenery. 'At a very early age,' Jane Austen's brother
Henry noted, 'she was enamoured of Gilpin on the Picturesque.'

# Reason, Feeling and the Picturesque

As ever with Jane Austen, in *Sense and Sensibility* literary taste is an infallible guide to character. While passionate Marianne revels in the Romantic poets – Jane's favourite, William Cowper, especially – with all their love of wild, untamed nature and rejection of artificial constraints and values, Elinor, although also loving Cowper and rejoicing in the beauties of nature, is equally drawn to the more intellectual pleasures of 'simple and elegant prose'. And the leading characters' contrasting responses to the best-selling works of William Gilpin are revealing.

Gilpin's series of guidebooks on the subject of landscape and the proper appreciation of art and nature had done much to influence a generation and inspire travellers both to observe and paint scenery with a new discernment. They were among Jane Austen's favourite reading: 'At an early age she was enamoured of Gilpin on the Picturesque,' her brother Henry recorded. Gilpin's rules on the 'Picturesque' – meaning 'the kind of beauty which would look agreeable in a picture' – so central to *Sense and Sensibility*, are also mentioned in her next published novel, *Pride and Prejudice*. Among other principles, such as the need to frame a scene with an overhanging tree or foliage, Gilpin ruled that figures in a landscape should never be depicted in even numbers but as irregular groups, ideally of three or five. In *Pride and Prejudice*, invited by Mr Darcy to walk with him and Mr Bingley's two sisters, Elizabeth Bennet responds laughingly: 'No, no, stay where you are. — You are charmingly group'd. ... The picturesque would be spoilt by admitting a fourth. Good bye!' Even as a devotee of Gilpin, Jane could see the funny side of his all-prevailing cult.

## Professional Success

At the end of October 1811, *Sense and Sensibility: A Novel In Three Volumes, By a Lady* was finally published by the London firm of Thomas Egerton, in a small edition of some 750 copies, priced at 15 shillings a set. Although she had determinedly withheld her name from the work, Jane Austen was now, at the age of thirty-five, at last a recognised, published author. It was a role she relished. While correcting proofs in May, she had told Cassandra: 'I am never too busy to think of S&S. I can no more forget it, than a mother can forget her sucking child.' She had no great confidence in her book's likely reception from the public: under her contract, she was to reimburse the publisher if sales did not cover the printing costs, and had set aside money to cover 'the expected loss'. In the event, *Sense and Sensibility* had something of a success. Reviewers found it 'a genteel, well-written novel', praising the 'pleasing narrative', and in aristocratic circles it was much talked of. 'Tho' it ends stupidly, I was much amused by it,' commented Lady Bessborough, mother of Lord Byron's future mistress, Lady Caroline Lamb.

And Jane would surely have been astonished, and touched, had she known of one particularly striking response, from no less than the Prince Regent's daughter, the fifteen-year-old Princess Charlotte of Wales. An only child – her mother, Princess Caroline of Brunswick, and the Prince Regent having been estranged since her birth – Charlotte was a sweet-natured but somewhat hoydenish girl, badly educated and given to impulsive acts. She was, however, fond of reading, especially poetry and novels, and she found 'Sence & Sensibility' (as she spelt it) 'interesting', a word then used with the stronger meaning than

Princess Charlotte
Augusta of Wales
and Prince Leopold
of Saxe-Coburg
William Thomas Fry,
after George Dawe, 1817
The only child of the
Prince Regent, and
heiress-presumptive
to the throne, Charlotte
was an early admirer
of *Sense and Sensibility*

now of 'engaging' or 'involving'. 'I think Maryanne [sic] & me
are very like in *disposition*,' she wrote thoughtfully. 'The same
imprudence, &c.' It would be one of the great tragedies of history
when, in November 1817, not long after Jane Austen's own
death, Charlotte died giving birth to a stillborn son after a year
of married happiness with Prince Leopold of Saxe-Coburg,
future King of the Belgians, and beloved uncle of Charlotte's
replacement as Britain's Queen: Victoria.

## Popularity and Privacy

The satisfaction of seeing her work in print was the encouragement Jane needed to resume work on another of her old manuscripts. Its original title, 'First Impressions', had unfortunately been used in the interim by another author, and it was to her beloved Fanny Burney that she now turned, choosing instead *Pride and Prejudice* from the line in *Cecilia*: 'The whole of this unfortunate business ... has been the result of PRIDE, and PREJUDICE.' Since the original manuscripts no longer exist, it is impossible to tell what revisions Jane made, but she reported that she had 'lop't & crop't' extensively, before submitting the final version of what would come to be regarded as one of the greatest masterpieces in English literature to the same publisher, Egerton – who paid the sum of £110 for it. 'I would rather have had £150, but we could not both be pleased,' Jane wrote dryly. In January 1813 she was able to report: 'I have got my own darling child from London,' as the first copy arrived and was read aloud at Chawton by Mrs Austen.

After the initial elation, Jane professed to feeling 'some fits of disgust' with 'P&P'. This might, she thought, be because her mother did not read well, failing to capture the different characters' voices. Nonetheless, she mused: 'The work is rather too light, and bright, and sparkling; it wants shade' such as 'a long chapter of sense' or some 'solemn specious nonsense', suggesting, tongue-in-cheek, 'a critique on Sir Walter Scott, or the history of Buonaparté'. To have had Jane Austen herself anticipate, and forestall, future ignorant criticisms that her work is merely frivolous and fails to deal with great issues is not the least of the pleasures of reading *Pride and Prejudice* today.

**Frances d'Arblay ('Fanny Burney')**
Edward Francisco Burney, c.1784–5
A lady-in-waiting to Queen Charlotte, Fanny Burney was one
of the most popular writers of the age. Jane Austen took the
eventual title of *Pride and Prejudice* from her 1782 novel *Cecilia*.

In fact, the book was a critical success. Other great writers, from Sheridan and Southey to Sir Walter Scott himself, were delighted by it, as were readers; by November 1813 the first edition had sold out, and a reprint appeared, at the same time as a second edition of the slower-selling *Sense and Sensibility*. 'I have now therefore written myself into £250 – which only makes me long for more,' Jane wrote to her brother Frank in July. In the face of her growing popularity, her determination to preserve her privacy remained as strong as ever. During the initial

**Robert Southey**
Edward Nash, 1820
He greatly admired Jane's writing; she thought some of his poetry 'very beautiful'.

reading at Chawton, even a visitor who was present was not told of her authorship, and it was kept from her nieces and nephews for as long as possible. Henry's indiscretion in revealing her 'Secret' when he heard some titled friends discussing the book upset her greatly, though she generously attributed it to 'the warmth of his Brotherly vanity & Love'. Nothing ever seemed to dim her regard for this handsome, charming brother, whom she fondly – if, with hindsight, not always wisely – entrusted with handling her business and publishing affairs, and her visits to him and Eliza in London gave her much pleasure. The couple seemed happily married, yet when Eliza died in 1813, probably of breast cancer, Henry seemed to accept the loss with no great display of grief. 'His Mind is not a Mind for Affliction,' Jane commented judiciously.

Even at Chawton, 'the place most closely connected with her career as a writer', in the words of her nephew's Memoir, finding the time in which to write was not easy for Jane. The cares of housekeeping and duties to others – from hospitality to house-guests to charitable missions to local villagers – had to take priority over what she regarded as something of a self-indulgent activity, and there were piano practice and needlework to be attended to. A superb quilt, made by Jane with her sister and mother and mentioned in her letters, has been preserved. And the daily female business of sewing garments for the poor, mending stockings and making up fine linen handkerchiefs, undershirts and neckcloths for the men of the family, known simply as 'work', could never be neglected. 'I can command very little quiet time at present,' Jane wrote on one occasion; on another, 'Composition seems to me Impossible, with a head full of Joints of Mutton & doses of rhubarb.'

# Mansfield Park and Morality

Nonetheless, before the end of 1813 she had, she told
Frank, 'something in hand' that she hoped 'on the credit of P&P
will sell well, tho' not half so entertaining'. That 'something'
was Mansfield Park: her first entirely new novel (as opposed to
revision of an old one) since abandoning 'The Watsons' during
the Bath years. If on one level 'not half so entertaining' as Pride
and Prejudice, it is considered by some to be possibly her finest
work, treating as it does of themes that range from poverty and
injustice, duty, honour and religious faith to sexual morality
and, by implication, slavery.

For a writer of Jane Austen's literary technique, it can be no
coincidence that she chose 'Mansfield' as the name of the great
country house where her downtrodden heroine, Fanny Price,
is sent to live, at the mercy of her selfish relations and virtual
masters, the Bertrams. Mansfield was the name of the Lord Chief
Justice whose landmark ruling, in a famous test case of 1772,
had decided that the common law of England and Wales did not
recognise a slave as a person's property. The horrific slave trade
itself was finally abolished in 1807, after long campaigning by,
among others, the MP William Wilberforce and the industrialist
Josiah Wedgwood. However, British plantation owners still
relied on slave labour – as, we infer, does Sir Thomas Bertram

............
OPPOSITE
**William Murray, 1st Earl of Mansfield**
John Singleton Copley, exhibited 1783
Lord Chief Justice of the King's Bench, whose landmark judgment on the status
of a slave under English law almost certainly inspired the title of Jane Austen's
third novel, Mansfield Park (1814), in which slavery is a discreet sub-theme.

in *Mansfield Park*, with his 'property' in Antigua. The subject is handled with subtlety and nuance; but the implications, and the subtext to Fanny's sufferings as an exploited, powerless woman, are unmistakable.

A gross misreading that has, however, unaccountably attached itself to this great novel concerns the famous pun made by the anti-heroine, worldly Mary Crawford on the subject of debauched old rear- and vice-admirals, and their sexual practices. Her weak joke, 'Of Rears, and Vices, I saw enough', has in recent times been taken to refer to sodomy – in the context of the times, unthinkable in a work of romantic fiction (however profound) aimed largely at young, well-bred, female readers.

OPPOSITE
**William Wilberforce**
Thomas Lawrence, 1828
Evangelist, philanthropist and MP,
Wilberforce was a leading figure
in the long campaign for the
abolition of slavery.

LEFT
**Josiah Wedgwood**
After William Hackwood, 1922
Prominent industrialist, owner
of the Wedgwood ceramics firm
and another ardent campaigner
against slavery. Jane Austen visited
the Wedgwood shop in London
several times to buy china. This
white jasper medallion of the great
man was cast from an original
Wedgwood mould in 1922.

In 1807, Jane Austen wrote that she had returned a novel by
Mme de Genlis to the library, with the words: 'We were disgusted
within twenty pages … it has indelicacies which disgrace a pen
hitherto so pure.' That she would even have hinted in a work of
her own at a practice then considered so foully perverted that it
carried the death penalty is out of the question. The allusion is
beyond any doubt to the prevalent Regency taste for whipping:
'*le vice anglais*', a risqué topic for a lady's wit, but legal, widely
fashionable and familiar to any schoolgirl who might glance
in a print-shop window at the cartoons by caricaturists such as
James Gillray and Thomas Rowlandson, in which birches and
buttocks featured regularly.

## Plays and Players

Attitudes to sexual morality are further explored in
*Mansfield Park* in the amateur theatricals scenes, in which the
young members of the family put on the daring play *Lovers' Vows*
by Elizabeth Inchbald, in which virtuous Fanny Price refuses
to take part (as Jane's cousin Phylly Walter did at Steventon).
Drawing on her own memories of those acting days, Jane Austen
wonderfully evokes the bustle of costume fittings, scenery
painting and role allocations. In this instance, she endorses
Fanny's stance: the play is improper, and so are the opportunities
it provides for physical contact between unrelated young men
and women. At the same time, her own love of the theatre – and
Shakespeare in particular – is strongly in evidence: hearing his

............
**Elizabeth Inchbald**
George Dance, 1794
Novelist, actress and playwright.
In *Mansfield Park*, her daring
drama *Lovers' Vows* (adapted from
a German original) is judged
wholly improper for amateur
theatricals by the novel's
virtuous heroine, Fanny Price,
who refuses to take part.

**Edmund Kean as Shylock**
Henry Meyer, after Walter Henry Watts, 1814
After seeing the acclaimed young actor Kean
as Shakespeare's Shylock in *The Merchant
of Venice* in 1814, Jane Austen enthused,
'I cannot imagine better acting.'

**Sarah Siddons**
Gilbert Stuart, 1787
One of Britain's greatest tragic actresses of all time,
Mrs Siddons appeared as Constance in Shakespeare's
*King John* in 1814. Through a mistake over tickets, Jane
Austen's hopes of seeing her were not fulfilled.

*Henry VIII* read aloud, Fanny is enthralled, and the hero, Edmund
Bertram, comments, 'We all talk Shakespeare, use his similes,
and describe with his descriptions.'

Just before *Mansfield Park* came out in 1814, Jane reported
with delight on seeing a memorable performance by the
celebrated actor Edmund Kean as Shakespeare's Shylock.
'I cannot imagine better acting,' she enthused. 'It appeared
to me as if there were no fault in him anywhere.' She had been
deeply disappointed on a previous London visit to miss seeing
Sarah Siddons, the leading actress of the day, as Constance in
*King John*, through a mix-up over tickets, declaring: 'I ... could
swear at her with little effort for disappointing me.'

## An Ambitious Move

The first edition of *Mansfield Park*, some 1,250 copies, sold out within six months; yet Egerton, who had 'praised it for it's [*sic*] Morality' seemed reluctant to risk a reprint. By now, while enjoying the success of her work, Jane was expressing her growing frustration at the lack of financial profit from it. 'People are more ready to borrow & praise, than to buy,' she complained, adding ruefully, 'but tho' I like praise as well as anybody, I like what Edward [her schoolboy nephew] calls *Pewter* too.' The time had come to make a change, and she now set her sights high. For her next novel, Henry approached the most celebrated and successful publisher of the day, John Murray of Albemarle Street. From best-selling travel books to major poetry and fiction, Murray dominated the market. Sir Walter Scott, Southey and Crabbe were among his list of authors, and with the appearance in 1812 of the verse epic *Childe Harold's Pilgrimage*, both he and its creator, Lord Byron, acquired near-legendary literary status.

'I awoke one morning and found myself famous,' Byron wrote sardonically, and this was scarcely an exaggeration. The handsome, dissolute young aristocrat, with his flowing dark locks, air of brooding melancholy, scandalous reputation and brilliant talent, caused a sensation throughout Britain and beyond. The firm of Murray could not keep pace with the demand for his work: copies, it was said, were being passed out of the windows at Albemarle Street to the jostling crowds below, and traffic jams of carriages banked up outside the poet's lodgings in Piccadilly, as devotees craned for a glimpse of their hero. Women were said to faint on meeting him. Had *Sense and Sensibility* been written just after, rather than just before, 1812, there can be little

**George Gordon Byron, 6th Baron Byron**
Richard Westall, 1813
Best-selling poet and Romantic cult figure. When his epic
poem *Childe Harold* appeared in 1812, his publisher, John
Murray, could not keep pace with the demand for copies.

John Murray
William Brockedon, 1837
The leading publisher of
the age, Murray counted
Byron, Scott, Crabbe
and Southey among his
authors. Jane Austen
named the heroine of
*Persuasion*, which he
published in 1817, after
Murray's wife, who before
her marriage had been
Miss Anne Elliot.

doubt that Marianne Dashwood would have been in raptures
over Byron, the ultimate Romantic. Her self-declared
counterpart, the teenaged Princess Charlotte, certainly was.

Jane herself, predictably, took a more balanced line where
Byron-mania was concerned. After another of his great poetic
works, *The Corsair*, had appeared in 1814, she noted sedately:
'I have read the Corsair, mended my petticoat, & have nothing
else to do.' She was, however, highly conscious of the impact
that his publisher Mr Murray might have on her own sales and
profits, and in the summer of 1815, Henry, acting as her agent,
sent him the manuscript of *Emma*. For all the deprecatory tone
of her reaction, Jane's joy on learning that her book had been
accepted was unmistakable. 'Mr Murray's letter is come,'
she wrote. 'He is a rogue of course, but a civil one.'

## Advice and Insights

While writing *Emma* during the previous year, Jane Austen had had extra demands on her time and creative energy from two of her favourite nieces, both seeking her expert advice on subjects of the highest importance, to her, as well as to them: how to write a novel, and whom to marry. Jane's responses, as the strictly secret correspondences unfolded, provide us today with extraordinary insights into her art and ideas. Her niece Anna – a talented, lovable, but slightly wayward young woman – was twenty-one when she decided that she too would write a novel and duly approached her authoress aunt for guidance. Jane's responses were illuminating. Anna, like many aspiring authors, chose to set her story among the aristocracy, with whose ways she was not really familiar. Jane advised her on some details of manners, such as the proper form for introductions and the use of titles, but gently steered her towards greater realism, urging '3 or 4 Families in a Country Village is the very thing to work on', and directing: 'Let the Portmans go to Ireland, but as you know nothing of the Manners there, you had better not go with them. You will be in danger of giving false representations.' She helped with structure and dialogue, and was at pains to temper her constructive criticisms with warm praise. 'If *you* think differently however, you need not mind me' was her tactful summing-up.

With Fanny Knight, her brother Edward's eldest daughter, this inimitable aunt was similarly forthcoming when asked for advice on love and marriage: 'so very interesting a subject', as Jane observed. Fanny was Jane Austen's favourite niece, described by her as 'almost another sister', the highest praise she could bestow on a woman. Helping, without ever dictating, Jane commented carefully on the characters and qualities of the different admirers and her niece's varying feelings towards them. 'Depend upon it, the right Man will come at last,' she assured Fanny tenderly. Above all, she made clear, the only possible basis for marriage was love.

## Varying Views

Astonishingly, the delightful love story she was creating in *Emma*, at the same time, did not entirely satisfy John Murray. He agreed to publish it on commission, along with a second edition of *Mansfield Park*, after consulting William Gifford, editor of the *Quarterly Review*, who responded warmly that he had 'nothing but good to say' about the novel. Murray still seemed uncertain as to the work's merits. 'Have you any fancy to dash off an article on *Emma*?' he wrote to his best-selling author and friend Sir Walter Scott, when sending him an advance copy, adding, 'It wants incident and romance, does it not?' Scott, fortunately, thought very differently. One of the earliest and greatest of all those who, over the next two centuries, would become Jane Austen's devotees, Scott recognised the depth of her subtlety and the art of her naturalism. Describing her own technique, with her usual droll self-effacement, Jane wrote of 'the little bit (2 Inches wide) of Ivory, on which I work with so fine a Brush, as produces very little effect after much labour'. But Scott saw in her 'a talent for describing the involvement and feelings and characters, of ordinary life', which, he wrote, 'is to me the most wonderful I ever met with'.

**William Gifford**
John Hoppner, c.1800
Journalist and editor of the
influential magazine the
*Quarterly Review*, owned by John
Murray. When Murray, uncertain
of the merits of Jane Austen's
*Emma*, sent him the manuscript
for an opinion, Gifford replied
warmly that he 'had nothing
but good to say' of the novel.

**Sir Walter Scott**
Edwin Landseer, c.1824
The poet and best-selling
novelist was an early and ardent
admirer of Jane Austen's work.

## A Royal Encounter

A still more illustrious admirer of Jane Austen's work entered her life in the autumn of 1815, while she was in London correcting proofs and preparing *Emma* for the printers. During her stay, Henry became ill, and a fashionable physician was called for, who was also in attendance at the Prince Regent's London palace of Carlton House. Quite possibly at Henry's instigation, given his propensity for boasting about his literary sister, the doctor carried word to the royal household that this anonymous, but popular, authoress was then in town. The outcome was a request from the Regent's librarian, The Revd James Stanier Clarke, that Jane might present His Royal Highness with a copy of her forthcoming novel. The ensuing events and correspondence were worthy of Jane Austen's own comic fiction, and would indeed be translated by her into fiction with hilarious effect.

The Prince Regent, she was informed with pompous cordiality by Mr Stanier Clarke, had read all her works and kept a copy of them in each of his residences. She was now invited not only to dedicate *Emma* to the Regent, but also to pay a private visit to Carlton House to be shown around the royal library. Of the two singular honours, the latter would certainly have given her the greater pleasure; the former, she found uncomfortable. Her support for the monarchy and staunch anti-Republicanism did not extend to regarding the heir to the throne as anything but the debauched, extravagant narcissist he was. In 1806 he had sought to repudiate his wife, the former Princess Caroline of Brunswick, on grounds of her adultery, and when scandalous evidence from what was then known as the 'Delicate Investigation' into her

............

**The Prince Regent (later King George IV)**
Thomas Lawrence, c.1814
Dissipated, extravagant and irresponsible, the Prince
Regent was deeply unpopular. Jane Austen detested
him, but was obliged to accept his patronage for
*Emma*, and include a fawning dedication.

conduct emerged, in 1813, the newspapers had a field day. The Princess was herself a figure of fun: overweight, underwashed, uninhibited in her public and private behaviour, and – according to the solemn testimony of a male servant – 'very fond of fucking'. Nonetheless, she commanded enormous sympathy from the public, who saw her as a royal rebel and applauded her every move, which included leaking letters to the press. Reading the reports, Jane Austen was shocked: nevertheless, she wrote, 'Poor woman. I shall support her as long as I can, because she is a Woman, & because I hate her Husband.'

Faced with the honour of the Prince's patronage, however, like Elinor Dashwood in *Sense and Sensibility*, Jane had to accept the 'task of telling lies when politeness required it'. (Although she would, she assured her friend Martha Lloyd, be 'influenced ... by nothing but the most mercenary motives'.) Her initial simply worded dedication to the Regent had to be amended, with Mr Murray's help, to one of florid fulsomeness, from 'His Royal Highness's Dutiful and Obedient Humble Servant'. And her replies to the increasingly pressing and effusive royal librarian are models of diplomatic gratitude, even when he took it upon himself to suggest subjects for her next novels.

............
OPPOSITE
**Princess Caroline of Brunswick**
Thomas Lawrence, 1804
The Prince Regent's wife, from whom he became estranged soon after their marriage. A flamboyant and uninhibited figure, she was nevertheless enormously popular with the British people, who saw her as a royal rebel. When details of her scandalous conduct emerged in 1813, Jane Austen wrote resolutely, 'I shall support her as long as I can, because she is a Woman, & because I hate her Husband.'

One was for a historical romance based on the family of
Prince Leopold of Saxe-Coburg, whose engagement to Princess
Charlotte had recently been announced. The other would be
the story of a heroic clergyman, based entirely on himself.
To the royal history proposal, having mentioned 'such pictures
of domestic life in country villages as I deal in', Jane wrote
gently, 'No, I must keep to my own style and go on in my
own way.' To the other, she replied with an irony that only
her thick-skinned correspondent could have failed to perceive:
'The comic part of the character I might be equal to, but not
the good, the enthusiastic, the literary.' She did, however,
unbeknownst to Mr Stanier Clarke, take up this suggestion:
the result was a mock-synopsis, entitled 'Plan of a Novel
According to Hints from Various Quarters' – involving,
hilariously, all the tedious details he had outlined to her
as the ideal basis for a work of fiction.

............

OPPOSITE

**Prince Leopold of Saxe-Coburg**
Henry Edward Dawe, after George Dawe, c.1817
When Princess Charlotte's engagement to Prince Leopold
(later King Leopold I of the Belgians) was announced in 1815,
the Prince Regent's pompous librarian suggested that Jane
Austen might write 'an historical romance' about the royal
bridegroom's family – a proposal Jane turned down with
immaculate courtesy, but barely concealed mirth.

............
**John Nash**
George Cruikshank, 1824
Among the greatest of all British architects, Nash was one of the designers of the Prince
Regent's London palace of Carlton House, which Jane Austen visited by royal invitation in 1815.

# At Carlton House

Jane Austen's impressions of her visit to Carlton House were, sadly, not recorded, but with her 'simple and neat' taste, she must have found little to her personal liking in the profusion of fabulously extravagant furniture, clocks, carpets, porcelain, paintings and light fittings amassed within. However, sightseeing – of houses as well as scenery – had been a notable feature of her novels, from Elizabeth Bennet's visit, as a tourist, to Mr Darcy's Derbyshire stately home, Pemberley, to Catherine Morland's projected trip to the Gothic fantasy of Blaise Castle; and the opportunity to see around this outstanding work, still under construction by one of the most important architects of the day, John Nash, would certainly have given her pleasure. Although 'making improvements' to property was a constant theme of her fiction, the only architect mentioned by name in her writing was not Nash, but the lesser figure of Joseph Bonomi the Elder, whom a titled friend of foppish Robert Ferrars in *Sense and Sensibility* proposes to engage. However, Humphry Repton is the landscape gardener referred to in *Mansfield Park*, whom Maria Bertram suggests her future husband should employ to remodel his grounds, and at Carlton House Jane would have seen, through the long windows, Repton's real-life work on the delightful palace gardens.

Even the Prince's patronage, the John Murray imprint and good reviews did not make *Emma* an outstanding commercial success, although the sales were satisfactory, with some 1,250 of the first edition of 2,000 sold in the first year. While most readers' reactions were positive, it was as well that Jane did not know of the opinion of one her own favourite writers, Maria

............
**Humphry Repton**
Henry Bryan Hall, after Samuel Shelley,
published by Longman & Co, 1839
Leading garden designer, famous for his
'Red Books', created to show clients the
appearance of their grounds before and
after his proposed transformations. Jane
would have seen his work on the gardens
at Carlton House during her visit.

............
**Maria Edgeworth**
Richard Beard, 1841
Jane thought highly of this acclaimed and popular
Irish novelist, though the admiration, sadly, was
not mutual. Miss Edgeworth is seen here in later
life in a remarkable, very early photograph – a
Daguerreotype by the pioneering photographer
Richard Beard, who opened a chain of studios
in London in 1841, the year of this portrait.

Edgeworth, to whom she sent a presentation copy. 'I have
made up my mind to like no Novels really, but Miss Edgeworth's,
Yours & my own,' Jane had written engagingly to her aspiring
authoress niece Anna in 1814, but the regard unfortunately was
not mutual. 'There was no story in it,' was Miss Edgeworth's
critical private view of Emma.

# The Final Phase

In August 1815, Jane began work on what was to be her last completed novel. She was approaching her fortieth birthday, apparently in good health and spirits, and in one of her delightful in-jokes, since this work was to be offered to John Murray, she gave the heroine the name of his own wife, who before her marriage had been Miss Anne Elliot. *Persuasion*, as it would eventually be titled, brought together many themes and strands from Jane's own life experiences, with its scenes set in both Bath and Lyme Regis, and, above all, its representations of the officers of the Royal Navy, whose unpretentious honour, gallantry and worth are her salute to her own beloved brothers and their service. There is an elegiac quality to *Persuasion*, and it was while engaged in writing it that the first symptoms of her terminal illness became apparent. The skin discoloration, stomach disorders, weakness and depression characteristic of Addison's disease were setting in, and before the first version of the manuscript was completed, Jane felt her powers failing. Dissatisfied with the closing chapters, she rewrote the ending.

Along with increasing illness, 1816 – the last full year of Jane Austen's life – brought her other sources of stress and worry. The aftermath of the Battle of Waterloo had seen an alarming downturn in Britain's economy, and in the spring of that year her hapless brother Henry's latest business venture, a bank with a branch in Alton, near Chawton, failed. He was left bankrupt, and among the investors who also suffered were not only rich relations, such as Mr Leigh-Perrot, but also Henry's French housekeeper, Mme Bigeon, and Jane herself, who lost £13. There was alarm of another kind for their brother Charles, whose ship HMS *Phoenix* was lost at sea in February. Mercifully, there was no loss of life, but Charles still had to face an obligatory court martial, at which, fortunately, he was exonerated.

With customary fortitude, Jane continued to apply herself to her daily household duties and her writing. The manuscript of 'Susan' was finally bought back from the firm of Crosby. Henry had much satisfaction, having retrieved it, in informing the obstructive publisher who the author was. Jane began revising the work, changing the heroine's name to Catherine and adding a preface to explain its long-delayed appearance. By the beginning of 1817 she had also embarked on a new novel, set in a seaside resort, entitled 'Sanditon'. Despite some fine passages, 'Sanditon' bore little promise of becoming another masterpiece, and in March the manuscript, amounting to some 24,000 words, was laid aside, never to be resumed in her lifetime. On 23 March, she confessed to her niece Fanny: 'I certainly have not been well for many weeks.'

A cure was still hoped for. A specialist was found in Winchester and in May, accompanied by Cassandra, Jane Austen left Chawton for the last time to be under his care. Despite her physical weakness, her mind and sense of humour were as acute as ever. She wrote with pleasure of their 'very comfortable lodgings' in College Street, Winchester, and her last letters were full of jokes, along with deeply moving expressions of gratitude for 'the anxious affection of her family'. In the early hours of 18 July, with her head pillowed on Cassandra's lap, she died.

Even in death, Jane's anonymity was for some time protected. The first few small newspaper notices made no mention of her writing; nor does the black marble tombstone in Winchester Cathedral, beneath which, on 24 July 1817, she was quietly buried. 'I have lost a Treasure, such a sister, such a friend as never can have been surpassed,' Cassandra wrote.

Yet today, two centuries later, to millions of readers throughout the world Jane Austen is a treasure, a sister and a friend.

**Jane Austen**
Cassandra Austen, 1804
A watercolour of Jane by her sister, preserved by the family.

# SELECT BIBLIOGRAPHY

Austen-Leigh, James Edward, *A Memoir of Jane Austen* (Folio Society, London, 1997)

Butler, Marilyn, *Jane Austen and the War of Ideas* (Oxford University Press, Oxford, 1975)

Byrde, Penelope, *A Frivolous Distinction: Fashion and Needlework in the Works of Jane Austen* (Bath City Council, Bath, 1986)

Byrne, Paula, *The Real Jane Austen: A Life in Small Things* (Harper Press, London, 2013)

Cecil, Lord David, *A Portrait of Jane Austen* (Constable, London, 1978)

Chapman, R.W. (ed.), *Jane Austen's Letters* (Oxford University Press, Oxford, 1979)

Copeland, Edward and McMaster, Juliet (eds), *The Cambridge Companion to Jane Austen* (Cambridge University Press, Cambridge, 1997)

Edwards, Anne-Marie, *In the Steps of Jane Austen* (BBC Publications, London, 1979)

Fergus, Jan, *Jane Austen: A Literary Life* (St Martin's Press, New York, 1991)

Gammie, Ian and Derek McCulloch, *Jane Austen's Music* (Corda Music Publications, St Albans, 1996)

Grey, J. David (ed.), *The Jane Austen Handbook* (Athlone Press, London, 1986)

Hickman, Peggy, *A Jane Austen Household Book* (David & Charles, Newton Abbot, 1977)

Hill, Constance, *Jane Austen, Her Homes and Her Friends* (John Lane, London, 1902)

Holmes, Richard, *The Romantic Poets and their Circle* (National Portrait Gallery Publications, London, 2013)

— (ed.), *William Godwin: Memoirs of the Author of a Vindication of the Rights of Woman, 1798* (Penguin Classics, London, 1987)

Honan, Park, *Jane Austen: Her Life* (Weidenfeld & Nicolson, London, 1987)

Jenkins, Elizabeth, *Jane Austen* (Victor Gollancz, London, 1938)

Kelly, Helena, *Jane Austen: The Secret Radical* (Icon Books, London, 2016)

Kelly, Ian, *Beau Brummell: The Ultimate Dandy* (Hodder & Stoughton, London, 2005)

Lane, Maggie, *Jane Austen's Family* (Robert Hale, London, 1984)

Laski, Marghanita, *Jane Austen and Her World* (Thames & Hudson, London, 1997)

Laver, James, *Costume and Fashion* (Thames & Hudson, London, 1995)

Le Faye, Deirdre (ed.), *Jane Austen's Letters* (Oxford University Press, Oxford, 1995)

— (ed.) *Jane Austen: A Family Record* (The British Library, London, 1989)

— *Jane Austen's 'Outlandish Cousin'* (The British Library, London, 2002)

MacCarthy, Fiona, *Byron: Life and Legend* (Faber & Faber, London, 2002)

Nokes, David, *Jane Austen: A Life* (Fourth Estate, London, 1997)

Parissien, Steven, *Regency Style* (Phaidon, London, 1992)

Ross, Josephine, *Jane Austen: A Companion* (John Murray, London, 2002)

Selwyn, David, *Jane Austen and Leisure* (Hambledon Press, London, 1999)

Shields, Carol, *Jane Austen* (Weidenfeld & Nicolson, London, 2001)

Southam, Brian, *Jane Austen: The Critical Heritage* (Routledge, London, 1968)

— *Jane Austen and the Navy* (Hambledon & London, London, 2000)

Stone, Lawrence, *The Family, Sex and Marriage in England, 1500–1800* (Penguin, Harmondsworth, 1990)

Todd, Janet, *Mary Wollstonecraft: A Revolutionary Life* (Orion, London, 2000)

Tomalin, Claire, *Jane Austen: A Life* (Viking, London, 1997)

Tompkins, J.M.S., *The Popular Novel in England, 1770–1800* (Methuen, London, 1969)

MAJOR WORKS BY JANE AUSTEN

*Sense and Sensibility* (London, 1811)

*Pride and Prejudice* (London, 1813)

*Mansfield Park* (London, 1814)

*Emma* (London, 1815)

*Northanger Abbey* (London, 1817)

*Persuasion* (London, 1817)

# LIST OF ILLUSTRATIONS

p.101 The Prince Regent (later King George IV), Thomas Lawrence, c.1814. Oil on canvas, 914 x 711mm. © National Portrait Gallery, London (NPG 123)

p.102 Princess Caroline of Brunswick, Thomas Lawrence, 1804. Oil on canvas, 1403 x 1118mm. © National Portrait Gallery, London (NPG 244)

p.105 Prince Leopold of Saxe-Coburg, Henry Edward Dawe, after George Dawe, c.1817. Mezzotint, 442 x 349mm. © National Portrait Gallery, London (NPG D45791)

p.106 John Nash, George Cruikshank, 1824. Etching, 340 x 248mm. © National Portrait Gallery, London (NPG D3010)

p.108 (left) Humphry Repton, Henry Bryan Hall, after Samuel Shelley, published by Longman & Co., 1839. Stipple and line engraving, 226 x 150mm. © National Portrait Gallery, London (NPG D5801)

p.108 (right) Maria Edgeworth, Richard Beard, 1841. Daguerreotype, 54 x 44mm. © National Portrait Gallery, London (NPG P5)

p.111 Jane Austen, Cassandra Austen, 1804. Watercolour. Granger Historical Picture Archive/Alamy

p.120 Silhouette, possibly Jane Austen, unknown artist, c.1810–15. Hollow-cut silhouette, 102 x 80mm. © National Portrait Gallery, London (NPG 3181)

## ACKNOWLEDGEMENTS

I am deeply grateful to Christopher Tinker, Nicola Saunders, Ruth Müller-Wirth, Hattie Clarke and Mark Lynch in the publications team at the National Portrait Gallery, and to Fiona Smith, the Gallery's Adult Programmes Manager. Others to whom I am indebted are copy-editor Helen Armitage, proofreader Patricia Burgess, indexer Lisa Footitt and designers Emma and Alex Smith at Smith & Gilmour.

My special thanks are also due to Clare Alexander, Andrew Clover, Robin Muir, Fergus Poncia, Timothy Ross and Rollo Webb.

# INDEX

Note: page numbers in **bold** refer to captions.

**Silhouette, possibly Jane Austen**
Unknown artist, c.1810 15